HOW THE HOLY FIRE
CAME TO AMERICA

Dee Kelley, Simeon Kwon and Other Humble Firebearers

Foreword by Frederica Mathewes-Green

Published by Felicity Press
Linthicum, MD
www.frederica.com

ISBN-13: 978-1977872982 (Color edition)
ISBN-13: 978-1978203464 (Black and White edition)

Book Design and Formatting: Simeon Kwon
Front Cover Photo: Candles of the Holy Fire, courtesy of Dee Kelley
Back Cover Photo: Candle stand with the Holy Fire at Joy of All Who Sorrow, courtesy of Michael Theophan Lujan of Joy of All Who Sorrow (OCA), Culver City, CA

Contents

Foreword:
United by Holy Fire

By Frederica Mathewes-Green
Holy Cross Antiochian Orthodox Church
Linthicum, Maryland

This is the story of a reverse pilgrimage. Instead of packing our bags to visit the site of a miracle, the miracle came to us.

On Holy Saturday, April 15, 2017, the Holy Fire descended on the Church of the Holy Resurrection in Jerusalem. It does this every year; eyewitness accounts of the miracle, even some by Muslims, go back to the 9th century.

On Holy and Great Saturday every year, the Patriarch of Jerusalem is sealed inside the "edicule," the small structure containing the place where Jesus' body was laid, which is itself contained within the immense Church of the Resurrection. While he prays, a blue light

The edicule of the Holy Sepulchre

emerges from the Lord's resting place, and fills the air. The Patriarch lights his candles from it, then comes out and presents the Holy Fire to the thousands of jubilant worshippers within the larger church, surrounding the edicule. They light their candles from his, and as the flame is passed from one person to the next, the fire goes rippling back across the room.

But this is no ordinary fire. Some in the room see their candles light spontaneously, without any contact with the fire. Bursts of blue flame are seen overhead. The Holy Fire is, at first, a mysteriously cool fire; while ordinary fire has a temperature of about 1000 degrees Fahrenheit, the Holy Fire initially burns at about 50 degrees Fahrenheit. People hold lit candles against their faces, and are not burned, but feel instead gentle waves of warmth. When hair or clothing is placed in the fire, it does not ignite. (Many capture this phenomenon on their cell phones, and you can see the videos online.) The coolness of the Holy Fire continues for about a half-hour, and then it assumes the characteristics of ordinary fire.

Yet it is still no ordinary fire; it is a fire that Orthodox Christians cherish. Many take the fire with them as they return to their home, even to other countries, to share with friends in homes and churches there. We call the women who came to Christ's tomb the "Holy Myrrhbearers," and perhaps we can call those who bring this fire to their churches and homelands, more simply, "Humble Firebearers."

On April 16, 2017, the afternoon of Pascha Sunday, a plane landed at JFK International Airport in New York, bearing two lanterns that contained the Holy Fire. From there, it was carried to several ROCOR churches in the New York area, and on Bright Tuesday it was taken south, to St. John the Baptist ROCOR Cathedral in Washington, DC. There, as you will read in the first chapter, Fr. George Johnson, of Holy Apostles ROCOR Church in Beltsville, MD, received the fire. The next evening, Bright Wednesday, he celebrated a moleben at his church, in which my husband, Fr. Gregory Mathewes-Green, took part. Afterward, he brought the fire back to our church, Holy Cross Antiochian Orthodox Church in Linthicum, MD.

Though the story, by this point, has progressed only three days, we are already in an alphabet soup of abbreviations, clerical titles, and Orthodox jurisdictions. It's not surprising that Orthodox Christians would swiftly come together to receive and pass on in the Holy Fire, but what we hadn't envisioned was how this sharing would bring us together across all ethnic lines.

Those ethnic lines are a legacy of immigration over the last few centuries. Upon settling in America, Orthodox Christians began building churches where they could worship in the language of home. They began establishing organizations and hierarchies to rule the church in this new land. As a result, there are at present some thirteen Eastern Orthodox jurisdictions in America, representing people of many different backgrounds: Greek, Ukrainian, Albanian, Russian, Carpatho-Russian, Antiochian (Middle Eastern), Serbian, Romanian, Bulgarian. Members of these churches may come from yet other Orthodox lands, like Georgia, Belarus, Moldova, Finland, Lithuania, and Macedonia, while converts from European and other backgrounds have further increased the diversity of the Church.

Though these jurisdictions are separate organizational structures, they are all members of the same world-wide Orthodox Church. They share communion and a common faith. The various jurisdictions might be compared to Roman Catholic parishes of the 19th century, where one congregation might be predominantly Irish, one Italian, one German, and so on.

In time, the various ethnic identities among Roman Catholics gradually became one; we hope that Orthodox Christians in America will one day be likewise united. While this happened naturally among the Catholics, for Orthodox it is complicated by the fact that each jurisdiction has established its own administrative structure. These are not easy to dismantle. Efforts to press for administrative unity have not had great success, and it's hard even to know where to start.

But an unanticipated effect of the arrival of the Holy Fire was that, across the country, people reached out to each other across jurisdictional lines. This took no committees, no resolutions, no official pronouncements; it just happened. Because Orthodox people share a love of God, because they share a common faith, they came together for the sake of the Holy Fire. They made connections with their Orthodox neighbors, perhaps for the first time—a connection that cannot be undone.

That is where David and Dee Kelley come in. They attended Vespers at Holy Cross Church in Linthicum on Tuesday evening, April 25, and afterward Fr. Gregory lit their candle with the Holy Fire. The Kelleys were just about to return to their home in Missoula, MT, after traveling in their RV for a year. As they considered their route along the interstates of the upper USA, they had an idea: Why not distribute the Holy Fire to Orthodox churches as we go along?

That story unfolds in the book you are holding now. Dee is a good reporter; she kept notes and took plenty of photographs along the way. A Facebook page, "Come Receive the Holy Fire!," was quickly established, which provided a place for the Kelleys and other "Firebearers" to share events and plans. A map of the USA was sprinkled with pins denoting those who had the Fire, those who wanted it, and those who were in the process of receiving it.

It was exciting to check in to the Facebook page and see the Kelleys' route, marked as a blue line, continue to move across the country. Before long, other Firebearers began to make their own similar journeys. Every day more pins appeared on the map, and every day more pins turned gold, marking a home or church where the Fire had arrived.

The unique value of the Kelleys' reverse pilgrimage is that their route took them through rural parts of America, making it possible for them to bring the Fire to churches that otherwise would not have it. Big-city churches get together readily, but the churches in small villages, the churches of the mountains and plains, are isolated by distance. As they drove along, the Kelleys kept trying to find Orthodox churches along the way. They did their best to connect with clergy or parishioners in these parishes, and were always willing to detour or to wait beside the road for people who had to come from a distance. They thought about how they could make the visit to their RV prayerful, making use of icons, incense, and recordings of liturgical chant.

Those who received the fire from the Kelleys sometimes went on to pass it along to other churches and other communities. Honestly, we don't know how far the Fire has gone. And there's no reason the mission of the "Humble Firebearers" ever has to end.

The unexpected blessing of the Holy Fire's pilgrimage across America was the connections it forged among American Orthodox of many different backgrounds. Those of us who have longed for Church unity in America can recognize that this is a greater and more certain unity, because it is based on mutual faith and prayer. Give the Holy Spirit a start like that, and there's no telling what can happen.

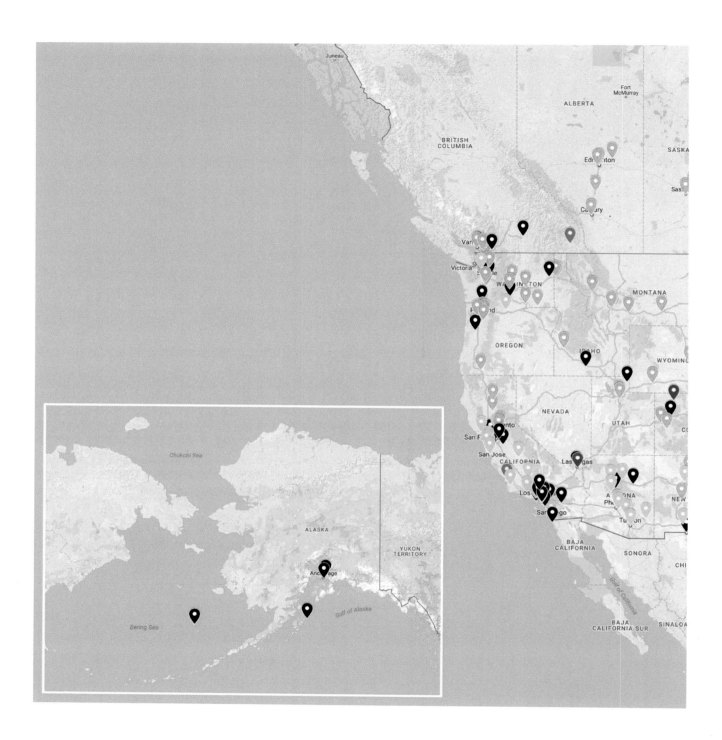

Map from the Facebook group "Come Receive the Holy Fire!" as of 9/17/2017.

I

The Journey Begins

The Holy Fire Came to Us

By Deborah Johnson
Holy Apostles Orthodox Church
Beltsville, Maryland

On Pascha of this year the Holy Fire arrived in America. It was Sunday, April 16th, 2017. The Fire had descended in Jerusalem the day before, on Great and Holy Saturday, in the Church of the Holy Sepulcher where our Lord's Resurrection occurred 2000 years ago.

In a historic first, the Holy Fire was officially carried to America and to England. In a miracle just as quiet, just as unnoticed by the world at large as the Resurrection of which it is a part, the Fire is now in the process of spreading all across our beloved country. Through God's grace, it arrived at my parish, Holy Apostles Orthodox Church in Beltsville, Maryland, on Bright Wednesday, April 19th, 2017.

My husband, Father George Johnson, is the rector of Holy Apostles. We had heard that the Holy Fire would be brought to America, but no details were known to us. Where would the Fire be brought? When would it arrive?

It was Bright Monday when I read on our Diocesan website that the Holy Fire had arrived in America, and was in New York City at the Cathedral of the Sign of the Mother of God. The article reported the itinerary of the Fire on the day of Pascha. The Holy Fire arrived at JFK airport and was greeted by Metropolitan Hilarion on the afternoon of Pascha, Sunday, April 16th. It was then taken to two Russian

Fr. George and Matushka Deborah

churches in New York for the Vespers of Pascha, and finally it came to the Synodal Cathedral of the Russian Orthodox Church Outside of Russia in New York City, also for Paschal Vespers.*

I contemplated the fact that the fire was near, only a couple hundred miles away from us, in New York. It was so close! This was a wonderful Bright Monday gift of grace. Throughout my 31 years as an Orthodox Christian I had longed to go to Jerusalem to celebrate Pascha and pray at the very location of our Lord's Resurrection, sharing in the joy of angels and men. I wanted to experience the Holy Fire, a Fire which is not only an external flame, but one which infuses all of Creation, making it radiant, on the Bright and Glorious Day of the Resurrection of our Lord.

I could not believe it when I read in the article that this great and hidden treasure of our Holy Faith would be made available to parish rectors during Bright Week! As Father George is the rector of Holy Apostles, we immediately began to make plans to go to New York and get the Fire, bringing it back home to our parish.

In the process of making arrangements to go to New York, Bishop Nicholas told Fr. George that the Holy Fire would be brought to Washington on Bright Tuesday! We didn't have to go to New York. The Holy Fire would be brought to Fr. Victor Potapov's home, where we could go to receive it. Fr. Victor is the rector of the Russian Orthodox Cathedral of St. John the Baptist, in Washington, D.C. We went to Ikea and bought three lanterns, and arrived at Fr. Victor's home on Bright Tuesday evening to receive the Fire.

We lit the lanterns and brought the Fire home to our house, where we lit our three home lampadas with God's Holy Fire. We scheduled a Paschal prayer service (moleben) for Bright Wednesday evening, and contacted our parishioners and as many friends as we could reach, to invite them to come and share in the Paschal joy, and to take the Fire with them to their parishes and homes.

As the service began on Bright Wednesday, there were a small group of people present, but they were representative of the Orthodox world, coming from different national churches and backgrounds: Russians, Greeks,

The lampadas at home lit with the Holy Fire.

Antiochians, and others. Five priests and a deacon, representing four Orthodox jurisdictions, were present at the service, where the Paschal canon was sung. All of the lampadas and candles in church were lit with the Holy Fire. I was able to put my hand in the fire over and over again. It was warm but not burning hot. Others present told me that they were also able to do so.

A sense of peace spread throughout the church. It was just as witnesses who have been present in Jerusalem have described, when the Fire descends in the Church of the Holy Sepulchre on Holy Saturday. Before the Fire arrives, people are chanting, "Give us the Fire! Give us the Fire!" As the Holy Fire descends from Heaven, the peace of God descends with it, filling our souls with gladness eternal.

On Pascha night, as Matins begins, we chant the hymn "Thy Resurrection, O Christ Savior, the angels hymn in the Heavens. Vouchsafe also us on earth, with pure hearts to glorify Thee." This year, we were able to glorify God in a new way, welcoming the Lord's Holy Fire into our little parish and our home. Along with many others, we Orthodox Christians will be touched by this wondrous miracle as it spreads across America.

When the Lord's tomb was found to be empty, the discovery was made by a handful of women. The event was announced to them by an angel, and the news spread gradually, quietly: He is not here. He is Risen! This Light of Christ's Resurrection is also spreading gradually, quietly, unnoticed by the wide world, as it travels to all the corners of our nation.

Christ is Risen!

* You can read about the first day the Holy Fire arrived in America on the website of the Eastern American Diocese of ROCOR (EADiocese.org). Enter "NEW YORK CITY: HOLY FIRE TO BE BROUGHT TO U.S." in the search box.

The Holy Fire arrives at Holy Apostles Orthodox Church.

II

The Northern Route
Like Wildfire Across the Great Northern Prairies

By Dee Kelley
Annunciation Greek Orthodox Church
Missoula, Montana

I remember watching a video of the Holy Fire in Jerusalem several years ago. I still remember the wonder and joy on all the faces of the people, the miraculous beauty as the fire moved throughout the sepulcher. Sitting in front of the computer screen crying, smiling, laughing, full of joy and wonder at this miracle.

And the joy of it never ends for me--I watch every year. I can hardly wait until the new videos are posted. Each year I try to share the experience with some of my grandchildren, to show them that God is still active in His world.

This year was no different. We'd been visiting our son Patrick and his family in Edgewater, Maryland, during Pascha. So I had three little ones to gather around the computer with me and watch. Together we watched the videos in awe, and as usual I cried. I know I am planting little seeds in their hearts.

I'm not sure when we heard that the Holy Fire was coming to America, but as soon as I heard it had arrived at an Orthodox church just 25 minutes away, I knew I had to go. On Bright Sunday, David and I drove in and we were greeted by a lovely Ethiopian woman named Aster, who was excited and joyous as she showed us the candles burning with the Holy Fire. We gazed at them like little children, smiling and softly laughing, with joy filling every pore.

After the service Aster gave us a candle lit with the Holy Fire, which she had placed carefully in a jar so I might take it safely to our son's home. All the way home I guarded the flame as best I could, but the long drive was too much for my little candle! As we turned at the very last stoplight, it went out in a pool of liquid wax. I felt sad as I watched it sputter out, but was still awed that I had actually carried that little flame. To have even seen it at all was a miracle!

It was time to begin the long journey home, from Maryland to Missoula, Montana. David had mapped out a route that we'd never taken, across the top of the United States. But I kept feeling a strong desire to try to bring the Holy Fire with us. What a joy it would be to have it in our church, even in our home! I prayed about this, and then asked David what he thought. He didn't need any convincing; he felt the same 'rightness' I did. So we decided to do it. We would try to take an open flame almost 2500 miles across the country! How crazy of an idea was that? But we felt strongly it was right, and that we should try. David contacted our parish priest, Fr. Rob Haralambros, and he gave us his blessing. So David and I joked that we were like the characters from The Blues Brothers movie long ago, "on a mission from God."

Dee Kelley receiving the Holy Fire from Fr. Gregory Mathewes-Green.

It took another few days to finalize our plans and gather supplies. After that, it was time once again to receive the Holy Fire. We arranged to meet with the pastor of Holy Cross Church, Fr. Gregory Mathewes-Green, after Tuesday evening Vespers. This turned out to be a double blessing as we were able to say hello to an exhausted Frederica, just arrived home from welcoming a new grandchild. So on April 25, 2017, we once again received the Holy Fire from Holy Cross Orthodox Church in Linthicum, Maryland. We carefully guarded the little flame all the way back to Edgewater.

As the few days passed before our departure, we began to think about stopping along the way to visit rural parishes and share the Holy Fire. It was being readily shared among city churches, but churches in the countryside were often far from those urban centers, and from each other. We didn't need to rush home; we had the time. So why not?

Once we made the decision, we realized that we'd have to have a number of supplies. Candles, lamps, metal buckets, sand...anything else? We looked around Amazon, and ended up ordering a tall 14-day vigil candle and two UCO candle lanterns, with extra supplies of candles. We bought two lanterns and lamp oil at Walmart, and two metal tubs at Kmart, and purchased a few tall candles at the Dollar Store. We thought we were ready, but we weren't. There was no way we could have anticipated what lay ahead in this unforgettable journey. We could never have imagined what God had in store for us.

We spent Saturday, April 29th making final preparations for the long, long drive. David and I spent the day loading the RV and getting our tiny car up on the tow dolly. It was such a beautiful day to be outdoors. Warm and sunny with a clear blue sky. After a few days of rain, it was a welcome respite. Our son washed his car with a little help from the grandson as our little granddaughter danced around the yard. There's such beauty in life's little moments like these. Normal everyday activities made special when done with love and joy in the heart.

The Kelley family prepares for their journey, setting up their trailer and car.

That night, we spent our last night at our son's home, with our sweet little granddaughter sleeping beside us. Early the next morning we snuck out of bed and, after giving the whole family sleepy goodbye kisses, we began the long journey home.

It was around 6:15 AM on the morning of April 30th, when we crossed the South River, heading out of Edgewater and on to Baltimore and beyond. The sun was coming up, and the soft light of dawn only hinted at the beautiful day that was to come. We were finally on our way! The Holy Fire twinkled in all of its containers-- two UCO containers in the cup holders, the 14-day candle in the tub beside the lanterns--all safe in the metal tubs with playground sand to keep them stable...or so we thought.

Did you know that good RV drivers try to stay in the right lane, because we typically drive much slower than everyone else? And did you know that the right lane is the bumpiest lane? Especially where it connects to bridges? No? Well, we didn't either! When we hit the first big bridge-bump in Pennsylvania, I thought I had lost some teeth! We had no idea how bad bridge-bumps could be, or how hard they would be on candles. One bump, and all the candles were extinguished! One bump! The minute we hit that bad one, the melted wax that had pooled around the little wicks sloshed up and extinguished every flame.

Bridge bumps are trouble indeed.

I was utterly horrified. I looked back quickly at the lanterns, and saw them sitting quietly, completely unaffected, and glowing happily in their sand-filled tubs! Glory to God! So we relit the candles and journeyed on.

The next lesson came the first time we stopped to fill the gas tank. We didn't want to have open flames around gasoline fumes (good thinking!), so we

10

The lanterns and candles all set up in the car.

extinguished the candles; then I got out with the lanterns, and stood alongside the building with my back turned, trying to shelter them from the wind. As David filled the tank over at the gas pumps, I thought that I must look pretty weird standing there with my back turned, with lanterns burning in the daytime, beside a case of bottled water (just in case). But no one seemed to worry about it, and nothing blew up. Success!

After fueling, David carefully swung the motorhome around to pick me up. Once I was safely inside, we decided to change out one of the UCO candles, which had gotten very low. We had lit them about 3 hours apart, so one would be going at all times.

When we looked inside the candle lantern, we saw that wax was everywhere, thanks to those bumpy bridges. David hopped out to get a screwdriver out of the vehicle's storage "basement." It took a bit of work, but we got the wax cleaned off and lit a fresh, new candle from one of the lanterns. Off we went!

We were both still a little rattled from the earlier candlewax disaster. A Facebook page, "Come Receive the Holy Fire!," had been set up for those interested in sharing the Fire and, as I looked it over, I saw many others had reported the same problem: candlewax melting and pooling, and putting out the flame. So we decided to use every resource we had: two lanterns in daylight, a large vigil candle, and the small oil lantern when parked! We had to make it 2500 miles, so we would need as much backup as possible.

You can see by the photo that we had the small candle lanterns in our cup holders. We had read about others doing this and successfully transferring the Holy Fire by having them cradled in the cup holders. The part they forgot to mention and I didn't remember (until it was too late) is that all the metal and glass around the candle lantern gets VERY HOT! As the cup holders are pretty centrally located, both David and I were getting little burns on our fingers as we moved them, but

the worst was when I accidentally put my forearm on the top of one. Now that hurt. David asked me if I needed him to stop and allow me to get an ice pack and I told him no - I was busy texting and making arrangements. I would get to it when I had finished. I don't know how long it was before he asked me about it again, but I had forgotten all about it. I had forgotten because after the initial burn, I never had any pain. Never! Glory to God! Now, healing it did itch a bit, but never any pain. It was simply a little miracle.

David with the Holy Fire.

I can't tell you how much the Facebook group, "Come Receive the Holy Fire!," helped us. Not only in helping us learn from others' experience transporting the Fire, but also in making contact with fellow Orthodox Christians along the way.

Though we'd had the idea of sharing the Fire with churches as we made the long journey home, we really had no idea how to get in touch with them. Facebook became our primary means of making contact with those who wanted to share the Fire. But we knew that wasn't enough, so we overcame our privacy fears and posted our phone number and email! I also decided that I would go ahead and phone churches, as we got within an hour or two of them.

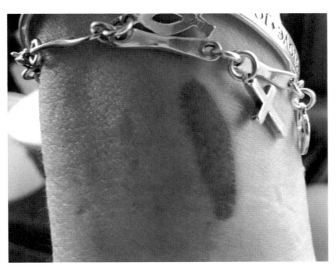

Not pretty, but pain free!

I used dear old Google to look up churches, and phoned to give them our contact information and ETA. This resulted in many phone calls to arrange meeting times and places along the way. Sometimes we had gone too far beyond them by the time we received a return call, and sometimes we didn't hear back at all, but it worked out pretty well, all in all. We were figuring it out as we went along, with no set procedure, no instruction manual, pretty much winging it the whole way.

There were many folks who were excited to hear of our journey, and wanted to know when we would be in their area. Unfortunately, we were unable to give exact times, for two reasons: the unpredictable effect of wind up ahead (which can really slow down a motorhome), and our commitment to wait for people to get to us. David and I agreed to make that a priority and wait hours, if necessary, so nobody who wanted the Fire would be missed. We also agreed that, if people lost their flame, we would turn around and go back (if it wasn't too far). In the whole trip we missed only one person, and it was one that really hurt us, because it was a sweet lady in her 90s who had gone to town, and wasn't home when we went through.

On Sunday, our route took us through Morgantown, WV. Thanks to my Google search I knew there were Orthodox Churches in the area. So I waited until church services would be over, and then gave them a call.

I was able to reach parishioners at Assumption Greek Orthodox Church, and we agreed to wait for them in a nearby Walmart parking lot. We parked and David headed in to pick up a few supplies, while I waited for the folks to arrive. It wasn't long before they drove up; there they were, dressed in their Sunday best, and there I was in my travelers' comfy!

This was the very first time we were going to share the Holy Fire, and I was so nervous I barely remembered to ask the gentleman his name. (Then I had to grab my notebook and write it down, before I forgot it!) When I saw that they had brought a candle, I shared the lessons we had already learned regarding those little darlings. One of their party went off to get a lantern while I lit their candle. I explained where the Fire had been obtained, and gave them instructions about getting out of their car and into their church without having the flame go out.

I had learned a lot from our Facebook friends, including stories about losing the flame as soon as a car door was opened and a breeze rushed in. I didn't want that to happen to anyone else. I watched anxiously as they transferred the Holy Fire into their waiting car, and waved goodbye as they drove away. I found that I needed to sit down and rest for a minute; to my surprise, I was exhausted! I had not expected that the blessing of this first hand-off would be as emotionally moving as it was.

Beautiful farms along the highway.

Before long David returned, and when he popped into the RV, he was not happy! "Did you get the tools out of the basement?" he asked. Uh oh! Well, it seemed our basement door was open, and the tools were gone! David was certain someone had somehow broken in and stolen them, while we were parked right there in the Walmart parking lot. I couldn't figure out how anyone could have done it, in broad daylight, in the midst of all the comings and goings in a Walmart parking lot. But we didn't have time to worry about it; we had to hit the road. And after the initial upset we had to accept that it was going to be one of life's little mysteries.

Wind. It is always the enemy when you drive an RV, or any big rig. You have to fight to stay in your lane, and unexpected gusts can be downright terrifying. But when you are carrying flames, there is even more danger. When you get out of an RV into swirling 30 mph winds, while carrying lanterns, anything can happen.

Our next disaster came at the very next fill up. As before, I got out with the lanterns outside the far edge of the station, and David drove over to the pumps to fill up. As he pulled away I did all I could to protect the flames,

You can't see the wind, but it's there!

but one huge gust hit and, poof! It looked like both had gone out! I looked up and saw that David was coming back around, and I ran to meet the RV. I leapt in the back, grabbed the long matches, and relit the small lantern. You do weird things when you panic, because I was so focused on getting that lantern relit that I didn't consider that my match would not be the Holy Fire! When that hit me, seconds later, I was absolutely crushed!

David parked the rig, and then came back asked me was wrong. After I explained the disaster, he said, "You didn't need to light it again; I'm sure it was still lit!" Of course, I thought he was crazy, until he showed me. If you think the flame is extinguished, lower and then raise the wick and the flame is there. David says it's because the flame remains below the metal where the wick is located. I'm not sure how he knew this, but he seemed certain and demonstrated it. I couldn't believe it, and I bet you can't either! If you watch the video on the Facebook page, you can hear my giggle when I saw that he was right!

But through the rest of the day and all through the night I worried about it. This "mission from God" was too important for there to be any question that we had kept the Fire burning every step of the way. While I knew in my heart that the flame had been present, I decided it was best to light the lanterns again. I didn't want anyone to have any doubts that this was really 'the' Holy Fire.

I poured over the map at "Come Receive the Holy Fire!," a map which was gradually filling with gold pins marking places that have received the Holy Fire. I tried contacting some of them by phone and email, and also asked the group for advice. Many sent helpful and encouraging comments, and one member even conducted his own lantern experiment and got the same result.

That evening we made it to Wolfie's campground in Ohio, and pulled in for some much needed rest. The beautiful Irises were in bloom, the lawns lush and green. The air was fresh after a brief shower of April rain. I was truly thankful we found such a beautiful place to restore our souls. God gave us a lovely evening in a lovely place.

The next morning I was able to reach Fr. Deacon Michael Walker, whose congregation had joyfully lit every candle in their church with the Holy Fire! We entered the address into Google Maps, and hit the road for Indianapolis and Joy of All Who Sorrow Orthodox Church. The little flames were still glowing, but I wanted to give them another touch of the Holy Fire. Double Holy Fire could only mean double blessings, right?

My sweet David successfully navigated our wide RV down the not-so-wide streets to the

Beautiful irises!

church. We were amazed to have found street parking fairly close to the church, but I was not going to take any more chances with sudden gusts of wind. I settled the small lantern into the sand inside the large painters' bucket, and covered it loosely with the lid.

Once I got inside the beautiful old church, I was glad we'd made the detour!

Fr. Deacon Michael invited me to relight my lantern from one of their candles, so I gently turned down my lantern wick (not all the way, wink wink!) and, using a taper, relit the wick. When I raised it again, the two flames had united (in my heart, both flames of the Holy Fire), and burned brightly in the little lantern. I thanked Fr. Deacon and lowered the lantern into the bucket again, gently placing the lid on top.

Then I went out of the church and into the WIND! Yes, the storm we'd been fleeing had caught up with us. I dashed to the RV (trying not to jostle the lantern), jumped in, and immediately removed the lid to look inside. A sweet little glow showed that all was well. I took the lantern out of the bucket and lit every candle and lantern we had. A sweet peace filled my heart; I sensed that all was right. The painter's bucket had become our best friend on that windy day.

Though the wind was definitely back, we now felt pretty confident that we knew how to protect the flame during fill-ups. From then on, when David let me out alongside the gas station I carried our trusty bucket with a lantern and two candles inside. Thanks to the hole in the lid, I could peer inside and check on them. When the candles needed air they would flicker and dim, and I could gently lift the lid, allowing a little fresh air in before carefully closing it again.

I must have looked pretty funny, anxiously tending my paint bucket outside a gas station. I caught several curious looks, but only one person came over to see what I was up to. He asked if there was something alive in the bucket--a fish, perhaps? Not exactly, friend, not exactly!

Icon of the Joy of All Who Sorrow to the left of the iconostasis.

Inside Joy of All Who Sorrow Orthodox Church in Indianapolis, IN.

We made it to Crawfordsville, IN, where we discovered 2 things: one, that there was an Orthodox church nearby, and two, they had the best pizza I'd ever eaten! We ordered delivery to the KOA campground that evening, and made our delivery plans for the next day. As I posted our itinerary on the "Holy Fire" Facebook page, Orthodox people in rural areas were hearing of our journey, and our delivery schedule was really picking up.

Best pizza ever.

We arranged with Kristin and Cody Boruff of St. Stephen the First Martyr Church in Crawfordsville that they would come the next morning to receive the Holy Fire. It was fun to see their initial hesitation as they approached the camper. We were strangers after all! And yet, once they ventured inside the RV, as we gathered in the presence of the Holy Fire, we became members of the same family. Distant relatives, maybe, but family just the same.

It was at this stop that David first began delivering his lectures--uh, instructions. He described every bad experience we'd had along the way, and delivered all the advice he could think of to help them get the Fire safely inside their church or home. (The Greek Orthodox church in Danville, IN, also received the Fire at this stop.) After my hubby's words of wisdom, we walked them to their car and sent them on their way.

Kristin and Cody Boruff with Dee Kelley (center).

You can see from the photo of one of our texts the careful method we used in screening and identifying the people we met with. Not so much! Just texts, phone calls, and sometimes a photo of the rig-- and then, smiling faces! Pretty simple, but it worked!

Next we met with Priscilla, who was taking the Fire north to Annunciation Greek Orthodox Church in Kankakee, IL. From there it would be shared with other churches. I think that was my favorite part of the journey: meeting all the volunteers who made sacrifices to meet up with us, receive the Fire, and make sure it continued to spread.

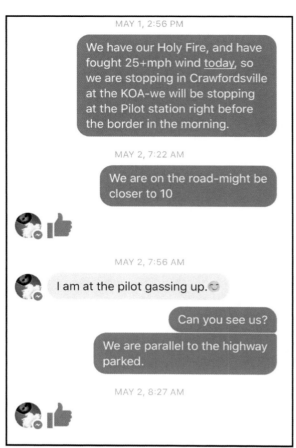

MAY 1, 2:56 PM

We have our Holy Fire, and have fought 25+mph wind today, so we are stopping in Crawfordsville at the KOA-we will be stopping at the Pilot station right before the border in the morning.

MAY 2, 7:22 AM

We are on the road-might be closer to 10

MAY 2, 7:56 AM

I am at the pilot gassing up. ☺

Can you see us?

We are parallel to the highway parked.

MAY 2, 8:27 AM

Instructions, as you can see! David was relentless in ensuring everyone got their little flames home safely.

Priscilla almost ready to go with the flame.

After saying our goodbyes, we were off to the St. Joseph's exit, where we would meet Christopher and Erin Soppet, who were taking the Fire to churches in the Champaign-Urbana area.

Christopher and Erin were such a delight! They came to meet us with their children in the back seat of the car and candle lantern ready. Their smiling faces were glowing with excitement and we were so happy to meet them. It was another example of how people approached us shyly at first, and then after just a few moments together, we felt like old friends. After their instructions and a little help getting settled into their car, we were all off to make our deliveries.

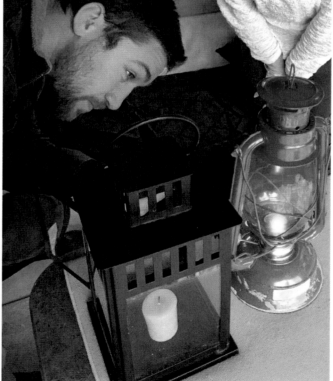

Christopher and Erin arriving to light their lanterns.

Around this time, David told me, "I have a confession."

"Oh, really?" I said.

"Remember when I got the screwdriver out, to clean wax from the little candle holder?" he said. "I think I just left those tools on the ground."

Now brothers and sisters, I didn't laugh, honest! Instead I simply said, "Well, I hope who ever found them really needed them, and were blessed by them." It was surely a miracle of the Holy Fire, that my mouth was filled that instant with the right thing to say! After that, I laughed and said, "If that's the worst thing that happens to us on this trip, I'll take it!"

So the great tool mystery was solved. We no longer had a bag full of tools, but we had hearts full of faith. We were still on our "mission from God," and knew Who was watching over us.

The gas tank needed a fill-up, and so did our tummies. What's the best road food for traveling up north? A Culver's Butter Burger of course! So we refueled the truck and then ourselves with that big, yummy burger! I was hoping calories didn't count as much when you are on a holy mission.

Our next meal in sight!

The drive through Wisconsin was beautiful, and we didn't encounter as much wind. And the cheese curds! Heaven! The farmlands were lush and green; pastures ready for planting

Beautiful green pastures and farms.

The beautiful landscape and trees.

On Tuesday evening, May 2nd, we were again blessed to find a lovely place to camp, just outside Janesville, WI. We weren't able to arrange any deliveries for this state, but we were kept busy making arrangements to meet people in Minnesota and North Dakota. The landscape was magnificent: the trees were just beginning to leaf, and the ornamentals were on their way to full bloom. The beauty certainly made it a pleasant walk when I took the doggies out for exercise. I was at least trying to work off those cheese curds.

The Holy Fire glowing ever so softly in the dark.

Every night I would wake up and go check on the Holy Fire. It was always softly glowing, with the little flames flickering gently. They bathed the whole camper in a soft golden light. It felt, to me, like waking up to check on a newborn and I felt a similar sense of wonder. Here I was in an RV in the American Midwest, looking at a miracle that had come all the way from Jerusalem. All the way from the Holy Sepulchre. By God's will we were chosen--commissioned--to take it across the top of the country. To the most rural of churches along with a few metropolitan ones as well! It was almost too awesome to believe. I have never felt so humble and blessed.

Our next delivery was planned to take place in the parking lot of a Sam's Club in White Bear Lake, MN (a suburb on the northeast side of Minneapolis-St. Paul). It turned out to be a great stop; we arrived early enough to have a rest, get a snack, and walk the dogs.

By this time, we had thought about ways we could make the experience as beautiful as possible. David set up our icons and lit the incense, and I began to play the beautiful strains of "Christos Anesti" (from the album Fire and Light by the choir of St. Symeon Orthodox Church) over the Bluetooth speakers. When folks arrived, we would encourage them to go in alone at first, to have a prayerful encounter with the Holy Fire. It was as appropriate a setting as we could make it, considering that we were traveling in a 26 ft. motorhome! And while it was the best we could do, I think it worked beautifully.

Our icon corner and incense.

The first group to arrive brought a nice tall glass container to protect their flame. Fr. Benjamin Ronald Tucci and James Varian came prepared with a nice tall container to protect the Holy Flame. It wasn't long before they were off to St. Mary's Cathedral Minneapolis (you can see that our doggies were always a part of the delivery experience).

Fr. Benjamin Ronald Tucci and James Varian with Dee Kelley (and doggie!)

The second group also came prepared, this time with a sturdy lantern. How I loved seeing young people come! How wonderful it was, to be able to bring kids along to experience this historic miracle. I kept messaging with C. W. (Mikhael) Lundin as we planned this delivery, and he was so helpful regarding our route, explaining the best way to avoid city traffic. He and his boys, Gabriel and Gideon, brought us an extra lantern, since they knew we had already given ours away. At the very next stop, we gave this new lantern away! We were amazed over and over to see how God always provided. One person would come with a gift, and the next person would need the gift. God's hand was evident in every step of this journey, in ways that amazed us.

Mikhael Lundin with his two boys Gabriel and Gideon.

The third group we met was planning to take the Fire to churches in the far northern regions of Minnesota, which meant traveling over smaller highways, after nightfall. Michelle Haapala, Alec John Michael Haapala, Deanna-Marie A. Nicholson Haapala had made quite the drive to meet us and we had a wonderful visit. It was humbling that so many people were willing to make difficult journeys like that, to ensure that their congregations received the Holy Fire. We had it so much easier, traveling nearly always on the interstate.

Here David is discussing candle safety and how to watch out for wax! Our friends had plenty of supplies to carry along on their long journey north.

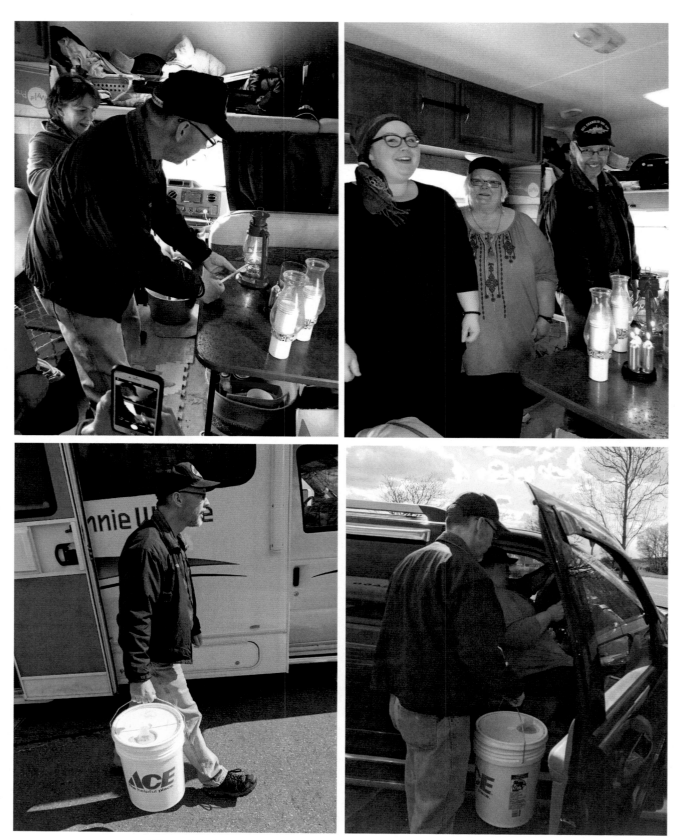

The third group receives the Holy Fire as planned.

You can see our trusty ol' bucket made a lot of trips from the RV to others' cars, ensuring that the Fire was transferred safely. And there's my gas station "peep hole" in the lid! That extra oxygen sure helped keep the flames going during long gas station stops.

These intrepid travelers delivered the Fire to St. Archangel Michael's Orthodox Church in Hibbing, MN, St. Basil's Serbian Orthodox Church in Chisholm, MN, and finally, Twelve Apostles Greek Orthodox Church and St. George Serbian Orthodox Church in Duluth, MN. Late that night, I got their message that they made it home safely before midnight. Glory to God!

As you can see, early mornings and late nights were certainly part of this journey. We anxiously awaited news from those who had transported the Holy Fire late at night. Thankfully, all made it home safe and sound. If you've ever driven small, rural highways at night, you understand. Deer, moose, road conditions and, of course, fellow humans make for some nerve-racking driving.

We knew to be thankful that there was little wind, so we got back on the highway and made good use of that blessing. When we stopped for the evening, I took pictures of the nightly routine of David filling the lanterns (we kept the refillings staggered, so both lamps could not go out at the same time). I posted the photo on the "Holy Fire" Facebook, page, and someone commented that it brought to mind the old gospel song, "Give me Oil in My Lamp." I remembered us playing that on guitar and singing with the children at church, in our long-ago Anglican days.

Did someone sing, "Give me oil in my lamp, keep me burnin'"?

We made contact with Fr. William Retting, at Holy Resurrection Orthodox Church Antiochian Mission in Fargo, North Dakota, and Google Maps guided us off the interstate and into town. After just a couple of wrong turns, we saw the church. It was situated on a cul de sac, which may sound fine to you, but it poses a problem for folks in an RV towing a car! We just pulled to the side of the main road, and used the dear old bucket to transport the Holy Fire inside the church.

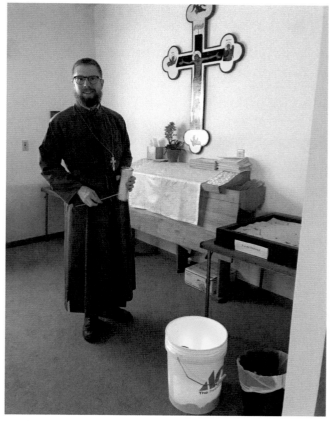

Fr. William receives the Holy Fire at Holy Resurrection Orthodox Church.

After a nice visit with Father, and making sure the Fire had made it safely inside, we started up the RV. As David started to make a right turn onto the street just ahead of us, I noticed it had a 'Dead End' sign. As you can imagine, it is not easy backing up an RV towing a car! I quickly yelled at him to stop, and then we weighed our options. We could drop the car and unhitch the tow dolly, turn around, and then re-hitch the car. That would take a lot of time and effort. Or we could take a chance on David making the small circle with the tow car and dolly still attached. We chose to give that a try; if it got too tight, we could unhitch them then.

After 44 years in a mail truck, David's skills were exceptional. He began to make the very tight turn in the cul de sac, while I filled the role of ever-encouraging co-pilot: "You can do it!" "Good job, honey!" "Almost there!" And then finally, "You did it! Great job!"

Whew! Crisis averted! That career mailman with his One Million Mile Safe Driving Award sure had the skills. As we headed back toward the interstate, we both felt relieved and ready to head to the campground for the night.

Just so you know, there aren't many campgrounds along that stretch of North Dakota highway. A few that we checked out turned out to be simply parking lots attached to motels. Those weren't for me, so we kept looking.

After checking various camping applications, my Allstay app came through with what looked like a good one; it had good reviews, too. But after we took the right exit and turned onto the access road, we discovered some bad news: we were going to be driving on a dirt road. This particular dirt road was crowded with pickup trucks, driven by folks who were anxious to get home after work; that meant they were driving fast, and our destination was shrouded in a red cloud of dirt. We continued about a mile down the gravel road (dear hubby was not happy about this), but we took it slowly, and soon pulled into an old, but well-kept, campground.

To our surprise, the place was very pretty and green. The sites were long and level, our favorite kind. God had brought us through the cloud of red dirt to a beautiful retreat! We took the mutts for a nice walk, then sat outside to enjoy the beautiful sunshine. It felt like we were on the last downhill stretch. There were only a couple more stops before we would enter Montana. The sunset that evening seemed to have a special western glow.

A beautiful retreat indeed.

The next delivery on our schedule was to Colleen Howe, who had often been in contact with us along the way. This sweet saint is a part of some of my favorite memories of this trip. She came to meet us in Bismarck, ND, along with fellow church-members Harry Kassian and Rebecca Perkerewicz. They came bearing gifts. The best part was seeing their heartfelt emotion--the awe and the wonder. The tears. As I sit here, I tear up just thinking about it.

They had come to bring the Holy Fire to one of the historic churches of the North Dakota prairies, a church Mr. Kassian's father had helped build. The congregations at these old churches are small now, but dedicated, and these devoted members brought us hand-made gifts and a lovely framed photo of their church. It restored our souls to have a nice long visit with them, and I hope we'll be able to visit them again one day. For now, the memories will do.

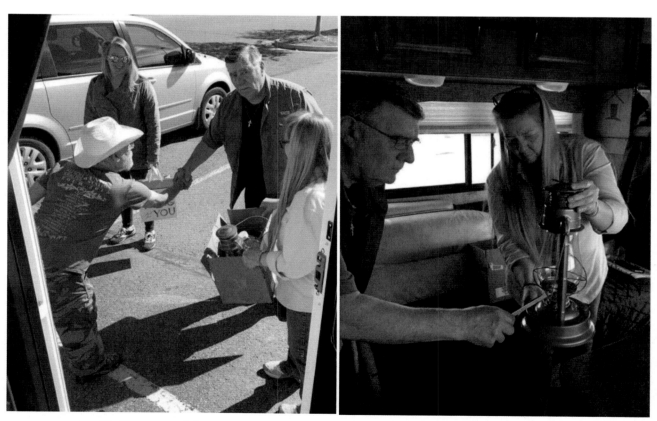

Colleen and her group arrive, ready to receive the Holy Fire.

I think I cried most of this trip-but at least I wasn't the only one!

What a sweet gift-which now hangs in my room near our prayer corner!

St. Nicholas Ukrainian Orthodox Church.

I got this photo of the church interior from their Facebook post, once they completed delivery at St. Nicholas Ukrainian Orthodox Church, Wilton, North Dakota. This church is over 100 years old and is simply beautiful. I hope to explore these prairie churches someday.

Our next stop was Belfield, ND; we had plans to meet Fr. Patrick Henre of St. John the Theologian, at the Walmart there. He and his family had come all the way from Rapid City, South Dakota--another example of the sacrifices people made to receive the Holy Fire. He also brought his lovely family along, and homemade cookies! These sweet, thoughtful gifts really made our trip. We enjoyed these treats the rest of the journey, and I still need that recipe!

After this stop, Montana was next! We were getting close to home. I was busy making arrangements with the Montana churches, and David thought we might even get home to Missoula in time for Vespers the next evening. I wasn't so sure, but figured we could do our best and let God do the rest. It was really His journey, after all.

Fr. Patrick Henre and his family.

The drive to Billings, MT took a long ten hours, and we had to fight the wind the whole way. By the time we arrived, we were worn out and both a bit grumpy (that's an understatement). The KOA in Billings, MT was the very first KOA in the country, and we'd always wanted to stay there. It is also located on the gorgeous Yellowstone River. So we decided to treat ourselves, and fork over the expected big bucks to stay there. As we pulled in, we saw that it was PACKED! After such a long, tiring drive, this was very discouraging. But we were already there, so we decided to see if they had a spot open for us.

They had ONE! And I'll let my Facebook post and pictures show you the miracle we received here:

 Dee Kelley ▶ **Come Receive the Holy Fire!**
May 6 at 7:29 AM

Another bit of evidence of God's hand in our journey. We drove a lot of hours and when we pulled into the KOA, we couldn't believe it but it looked full! We've hardly had any neighbors until now. But we went in to see: 1 pull through left. Only one! Of course, we took it site unseen. Now, look below at our space compared to everyone else.

43

I put my feet in a Montana river, and I immediately felt the most profound sense of peace. I was almost giddy with happiness and, of course, tears of gratitude stung my eyes. The canyon glowed with the light of the setting sun, and right that second it hit me how much this journey had affected me. How many people had God touched over all the miles? How many would He continue to touch, as folks from Idaho, Washington state and Canada were arranging to receive the Fire from

My feet in a Montana River.

our parish, once we made it home? It was so amazing and humbling, that this old sinner had been allowed to participate in such a beautiful event.

The beautiful canyon.

Early the next morning we connected with Fr. Moses Hibbard and Fr. Deacon Michael Norbury, of Saint Nicholas Orthodox Church in Billings, who knew exactly where we were, and drove over to meet us. Once again we were blessed with lovely, unexpected gifts--and one was another little miracle, as it made a perfect fit for someone we love.

As usual, David was anxious to share how to get the fire safely back to the church with Fr. Moses and Fr. Deacon Michael.

A copy of 'The Faith of the Saints' and a St. Nicholas Icon.

Fr. Moses had no way of knowing that one of our granddaughters would need this very book, but God did. The Sunday after we got home, our sweet granddaughter Katlyn told us she wanted to be baptized, and this book has been such a great resource for her! It is arranged in a question and answer format that is perfect for helping her learn and understand the Orthodox faith. Glory to God.

We spent a little more time here than we had planned, so after our goodbyes, we headed back out toward Bozeman. We knew that if all went well, we just might make it to Missoula--if not in time for Vespers, at least by the end of the service. David knew Fr. Rob wanted to present the Fire the next morning during the Liturgy. So off we went!

Safely delivered via little lantern and sand bucket-the Holy Fire was given a beautiful home at St. Nicholas.

The Walmart parking lot was once again our chosen meeting place, this time in Bozeman. When we arrived, Fr. David Morrison, of St. Anthony the Great Orthodox Church, was inside doing some shopping; he needed to buy a lantern and other supplies. He had brought his lovely daughters along, and we got one of my favorite photos from their visit.

What a special moment to share with your children! We enjoyed a short visit, but clouds were rolling in and we still had a lot of miles to cover.

We could see the mountains, but we were also seeing an increase in our old nemesis, wind! David had to wrestle that old friend once more, as we tried to stay on schedule

Fr. David and his daughters receive the flame!

and make it to Vespers. We prayed we could make it, but after all the miles and miracles we weren't too worried; we knew who was really in control. The miles went flying by, and finally we were on the home stretch.

The mountains were beautiful, but wind came not long after.

We made it to Butte, but it was so windy!

The clouds began to get worse, and we could tell a storm was approaching. As soon as we turned into the driveway of Holy Trinity Orthodox Church in Butte, MT, a big gust of wind rocked the camper! It had to have been a microburst; it was certainly the worst we'd experienced so far. We knew the little bucket was going to be sorely tested now. In the photo, you can see the dirt blowing hard across the parking lot, as the cloud lowered.

Fr. Russell came out to help us and carefully, through the howling wind, he and David made it inside. There we saw that the little lantern was sitting firmly in the sand, its warm glow safe and sound. We gave a sigh of relief, followed immediately by a gasp of unbelief, as we looked around at one of the most beautiful churches we'd ever seen, and here it was in Butte, Montana!

I could barely take it all in, though I knew we had no time to dilly dally. So I took a few photos and then we said our hasty goodbyes. David and I ran toward the camper, secured the little lantern in its bucket of sand, and were just about to leave when Fr. Russell knocked on the door. He told us he had looked at the radar, and there was a break in the storm; if we followed him, he would lead us to the freeway by a shortcut. Of course, we did exactly that.

Front view of Holy Trinity Orthodox Church.

49

Left wall of Holy Trinity Orthodox Church.

Altar of Holy Trinity Orthodox Church.

The partial dome with the Theotokos above the altar.

The wind was really beating us up by the time we hit the freeway. We prayed we wouldn't have to stop. As we drove, I saw a lighter area in the clouds to David's left--just a spot, an oval shape that was much lighter than the rest of the clouds. I pointed it out to him, and said I believed it was the back of the storm. We prayed to stay just behind until it passed.

The pictures tell the story of this miracle. Here was our view leaving Butte:

When we got closer to the storm it looked terrible, and we knew that, if we caught it, we would have to pull over and stop. Wind would mean the journey that day was over.

Here's the view to the left, middle and right before we saw the light in the clouds:

Then, suddenly, there it was-a light. A gap in the storm, as if a window shade was being raised just a bit. We hoped we were headed that direction!

The gap in the storm right there!

It was great we only had drenched highways.

We followed the light for miles, and never caught up with the storm. We barely even had any rain, just seemed to drive over drenched highway. But the light and its location didn't change much at all; it simply led the way, and we followed.

Finally, we came to the last turn to head into Missoula:

And the sun came out. God had escorted us and the Holy Fire home. We were awed and overwhelmed, and more thankful than either of us could express.

As we drove into the parking area at 5:45 pm, we knew God had opened the way for us and our little lantern to make it right before Vespers ended! We decided to wait and not interrupt the service, but I think people had been keeping up with us on Facebook, and one of the parishioners came to the door and looked out. The cat was out of the bag! Our fellow parishioner Andrew came out to meet us, and told us that Vespers was almost over. So David loaded the little lantern into its bucket for what we thought would be the last time. Thankfully, there was now no wind to speak of as Andrew helped David make the journey up the stairs with the heavy bucket.

We had been away from our little parish for one full year. We work-camped near Glacier National Park last summer, then spent almost 6 months in Texas visiting friends and family, and finally an amazing three weeks in Maryland with our son and his family. All these adventures had led us right up to this one special moment in time. I believe God ordained that David and I, our little camper, and our little lanterns would be in the right place at the right time to do this work, as he guided us all the way. We waited as quietly as we could, but it wasn't long before we were noticed.

We are so close to Annunciation Orthodox Church! Almost there!

58

The Holy Fire safe in the bucket.

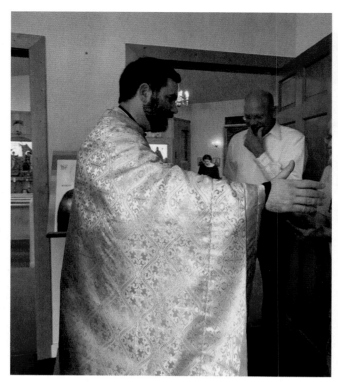

David gets a long awaited hug from Fr. Rob.

Fr. Rob's little acolyte was finally home, and their reunion so sweet. Of course, it made me cry. I'm becoming used to this crying thing...

One parishioner had come to see the fire because she was leaving town the next day, and so one lantern went home with her. Andrew had brought a marine-type lantern we could not get working, and so one of our donated extras went home with him. As always, needs were met before we knew they existed.

Plans were made to receive the fire the next morning during service, and so the little lantern went back into the camper and we drove home. We were greeted with shrieks of joy by our daughter and granddaughter, and were happy to sleep in our 'real' bed for the first time in a year! It was so good to be home.

The next morning the little lantern and the candles went back in the bucket for the trip to church. The congregation was excited to see us, after our long trip, but of course the arrival of the Holy Fire was much more exciting than we were.

My final Facebook post about our 2500 mile journey revealed the last and most fitting miracle of all: Fr. Rob's bundle of candles.

*Father Rob welcomes the Holy Fire to Annunciation Greek Orthodox
Church, Missoula, Montana.*

Dee Kelley
May 7

Today the Holy Fire was welcomed to our church-Annunciation Greek Orthodox Church, Missoula, MT. Would you like one more miracle story? Our priest received a gift a few years ago of a bundle of 33 candles-like those used in Jerusalem. He wondered what he was ever going to do with them-until today-when their purpose was revealed to us all. Glory to God! And we have parishioners coming from Canada and Idaho-the beauty and mystery of the Holy Fire continues even though our part of the journey has come to an end. Thank you for coming with us with your prayers and good wishes! May the Light of Christ guide us all into His kingdom-and yes-that's me crying again!

Father Rob sharing the Holy Fire with Rev. Deacon Mark Townsend of St. John the Baptist Antiochian Orthodox Church in Post Falls, ID

Our part of the journey was over, but as the ever-changing map on the "Come Receive the Holy Fire!" Facebook page reveals, the flame we carried is still moving along. It continues to be shared by the wonderful people who volunteer to escort it on this amazing journey. It didn't take long for Orthodox folks from Idaho to make the trip over, and then came the Canadians, ready to face the unknown at the border! Their journey kept us up late as we watched for updates, and gave us joy when they made it across. Calgary, Red Deer and then Edmonton; from there on the Saskatoon and Winnipeg.

Dianne Julianna Storheim-Hill
May 8

The Fire is in western Canada. On its way to Calgary, Red Deer, and Edmonton before midnight God willing. The travellers tell me they have been truly blessed thus far.   Pictures from Annunciation Greek Orthodox Church in Missoula where they received the Fire this morning.

More pictures of Annunciation Greek Orthodox Church.

The Holy Fire had journeyed with us for 2500 miles- from the Chesapeake Bay on the east coast, through the great northern prairies to the Rocky Mountains and Missoula, Montana. It then spread quickly to the west coast, and north into Canada. As I write the southern journey is underway, and I often watch often for updates on the map. The Miracle of the Holy Fire was once just an annual event we experienced via YouTube videos, from thousands of miles away. We never in our wildest dreams thought we would see it, carry it in our own vehicle, and deliver it to others. We never could have imagined meeting so many Orthodox Christians: Russian, Serbian, Greek, Antiochian, Ukrainian, all over the northern half of the United States. So here's a great big "Thank you" to all who assisted us along the way, from Fr. Gregory Mathewes-Green who originally gave us the fire, to all the volunteers across the country who made long journeys to connect with us, and to the administrators of the Facebook page that kept us all in touch. Thanks are especially due to Magda Andronache. This lady updated the map mostly at night, when her babies were finally down to sleep, but also whenever she could spare a moment. Her updating work continues, as the Holy Fire keeps spreading.

May God continue to bless His Holy Orthodox Church and His people. We now see that we are connected with each other more than we knew, for at a deep level we are united in a common faith. How right it is that this deep unity was illuminated by the pathway of the Holy Fire. From the big cities of the Northeast to the farmlands of Illinois and Indiana; from the dairy farms of Wisconsin to far Northern Minnesota; across the prairies of the Dakotas and western Montana to the mountains and beyond! We are one in our faith, and now linked with each other by the Miracle of the Holy Fire. May we keep this connection alive, and may the Holy Fire glow in our hearts forever. Continue to be His firebearers!

Christo Anesti! Khristos Voskrese! Khristos voskres! Christo vaskres! Christ is Risen!

APPENDIX

From Priscilla:

The only photo I have is my candle lantern guiding me back to Annunciation Greek Orthodox Church in Kankakee, IL. The 2 additional 10 day candles (with extra aluminum foil shields) and the lantern that you so generously provided, ALL made it to the church still burning with the Holy Fire. Blessings on you and all those who made this happen! As I watched the map grow each day, it filled me with joy and wonder that all of those receiving and passing along the Holy Fire are such a diverse group. We are converts and cradle Orthodox of all ethnicities and backgrounds. All languages, all orthodox traditions --- there were no borders! Exactly what our Orthodox faith represents has been played out and is STILL being played out as more people receive the Holy Fire each day! It is a truly wondrous moment to participate in and to witness! Glory to God!

---Priscilla Skala

Our pre-journey miracle:

While on our journey with the Holy Fire, we shared many miracle moments with everyone who followed-but one we haven't shared happened BEFORE we left. I'm sharing so you will see that God made sure we even accepted the invitation to carry the Fire. Here is what happened. David went with Patrick and Cody on a baseball road trip. While in New York, he fell and severely pulled a muscle in his groin. He was limping and in constant pain, but tried to keep up with the kids. They journeyed to Boston and on the way to the game they all went to the Orthodox seminary, where David wanted to venerate the relic of the True Cross. He took a couple of photos as he approached, and as he walked up the steps from the street level, his pain disappeared. He was healed completely, unexpectedly and miraculously. What he didn't notice until later was the light in the photographs he had taken. The blue light that is clearly visible and aiming at what would have been his groin area, from 2 different positions, is clearly seen. The Holy Fire is first seen as a blue light! David received his miracle, was instantly pain free and able to drive 2500 miles and deliver the Holy Fire. He likes to look at the Icon of the Annunciation as a reminder of how God worked in his life in such a miraculous way. Glory to God!

Hellenic College Holy Cross Seminary, in front of Holy Cross Chapel.

Facebook posts from the Facebook Page: "Come Receive the Holy Fire!"

 Kristin Baumann Boruff
May 2 · Williamsport, IN

Thank you Dee Kelley! We have received the Holy Fire in Warren County Indiana! Christ is risen!

William Basil

May 20

The Holy Fire has been received in Smuts, Saskatchewan

Sarah Henre

May 13

Can you please change the marker for Holy Resurrection in Gillette, WY?
They received the Holy Fire today 🙂

Dianne Julianna Storheim-Hill

May 14 · Edmonton, AB, Canada

The Holy Fire was distributed after Liturgy today at Holy Trinity Orthodox Church in Edmonton Alberta Canada. Glory be to God! It is a joy to see it travel across North America.

Leanne Parrott with Dianne Julianna Storheim-Hill and John Hans Pätkau.

May 11 · Calgary, AB, Canada

The Holy Fire arrived safely in Calgary, Alberta, Canada this week at Holy Martyr Peter the Aleut Orthodox Church (OCA), thanks to the hard work of our brothers from Edmonton who drove to Missoula to pick it up! Edmonton to Missoula is about 880 km or 547 miles.

Michelle Haapala
May 7 · Hibbing, MN

Christ is risen! We officially welcomed the Holy Fire to St. Archangel Michael's Orthodox Church in Hibbing, MN today. It was special! As far as we know this is the first time in history that the Holy Fire has made it to the Iron Range in Minnesota! Slava Bogu!

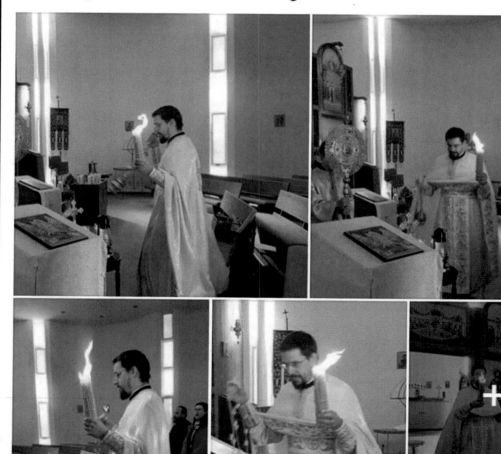

William Basil

May 11

The transfer of the Holy Fire from Edmonton towards Vegreville and then Saskatoon, Saskatchewan.

Athina A. Collins is at 📍 Annunciation Greek Orthodox Church - Missoula, Montana.

May 7 · Missoula, MT

Dee Kelley
May 6 · Billings, MT

First delivery of the day: Saint Nicholas, Billings, Mt

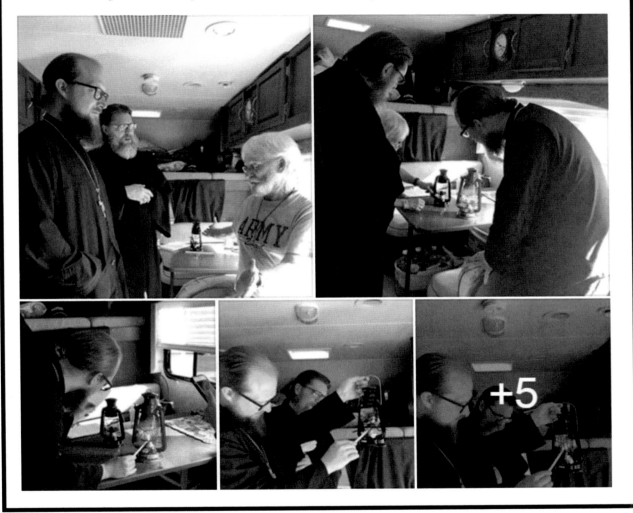

Dee Kelley
May 3

Deliveries! Michael CW Lundin, Alec and Deanna Haapala, Michelle Haapala, Carol Zakula: planning delivering to multiple churches including: St. Basil's Serbian, Chisholm, MN; Holy Apostles Greek Orthodox Church, Duluth, MN; St. Archangel Michael's in Hibbing, MN; St. George Serbian Orthodox Church, Duluth, MN.

David Kelley
May 6 · Dickinson, ND

Our 2nd delivery today was Fr. Patrick Henre, of St. John's in South Dakota. We were so blessed by this sweet family-who baked us cookies! Another great day!

Dee Kelley
May 4

Delivery! Holy Resurrection Orthodox Church, Fargo, ND! Supplies, gas, grub and a few more miles before we call it a day.

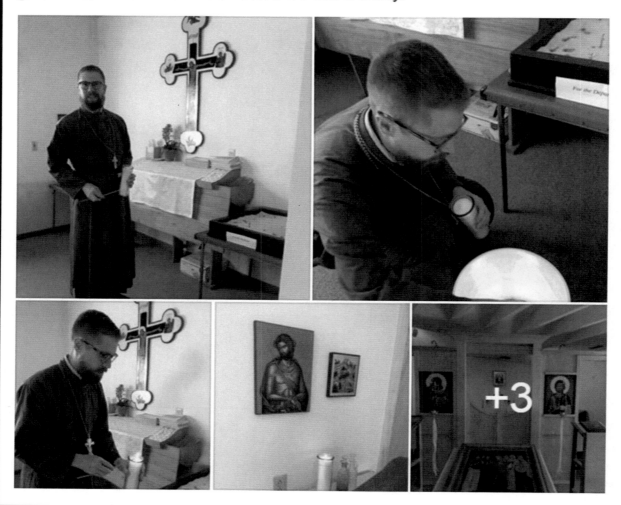

Patrick Henre
May 5

St. John the Theologian Orthodox Church in Rapid City has received the Holy Fire! Thank you Dee Kelley

Deanna-Marie A. Nicholson Haapala
May 4

The Holy Fire made it to Embarrass, MN after an 8 hour journey from the Twin Cities and dropping it off to the Northland Churches. Christ is Risen!

FrBenjamin Ronald Tucci
May 3

Holy Altar of st Mary's Cathedral in Minneapolis glowing with the Holy Fire.

Victoria Marckx
May 12

St. Demetrios Greek Orthodox Church in Winnipeg, Manitoba, Canada has the Holy Fire! (via Holy Resurrection in Fargo, ND)

Dee Kelley
May 6 · Bozeman, MT

Delivery! Saint Anthony the Great, Bozeman, Mt!

Dee Kelley
May 3 · White Bear Lake, MN

Delivery! St. Mary's Orthodox Cathedral!

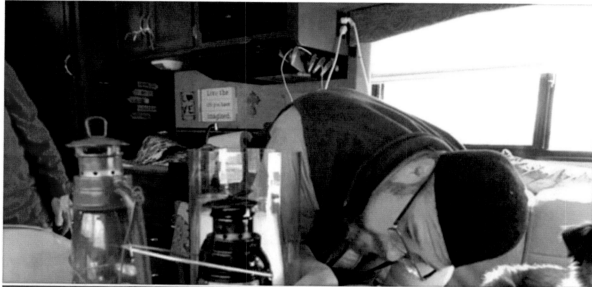

The route from start to finish.

1. Assumption Greek Orthodox Church, Morganstown, WV and camped at Wolfie's campground in Zanesville, Ohio. Relit the flame in Indianapolis, IN at Joy of All Who Sorrow Orthodox Church.

2. Crawfordsville, IN - camped at KOA in Crawfordsville and then met the next morning with folks from St. Stephen the First Martyr and another picked up to deliver to Annunciation Greek Orthodox Church in Kankakee, IL.

3. Danville, IL - where flame was picked up and taken to Annunciation Greek Orthodox Church.

4. St. Joseph, IL - pick up for Champagne, IL. Stopped in Edgerton, WI at Hidden Valley RV Resort

5. Hibbing, MN - pickups for St. Mary's Cathedral, Minneapolis, MN, St. Archangel Michael's in Hibbing, MN and a pick up from wonderful people heading to northern Minnesota to St. Basil's Serbian Orthodox Church, Chisholm, MN, Holy Apostles Greek Orthodox Church, Duluth, MN, and St. George Serbian Orthodox Church in Duluth, MN.

6. Holy Resurrection Mission, Fargo ND. Then on to Jamestown campground.

7. Met folks from Belfield, ND who carried the Fire to St. Nicholas Ukrainian Church. At the same stop we met up with folks from St. John the Theologian, Rapid City, SD.

8. Billings, MT spent the night at the FIRST KOA in the country! Delivered to St. Nicholas Orthodox Church next morning.

9. Bozeman, MT - St. Anthony Orthodox Church.

10. Butte, MT - Holy Trinity Serbian Orthodox Church. And skirted the mighty thunderstorm to arrive home in Missoula, MT at Annunciation Greek Orthodox Church.

III

The Southern Route
The Way of the Pilgrim

By Simeon Kwon
Holy Resurrection Orthodox Church
Allston, Massachusetts

The journey first started, by the grace of God, with the arrival of the Holy Flame in America on Pascha of 2017, which was April 16. Of course, I was completely ignorant of this fact as my parish celebrated Pascha at Holy Resurrection Orthodox Church in Allston MA. Being my second Pascha since my baptism, it was such an experience of grace to be part of the Paschal celebration.

After morning liturgy finished several days later on April 21st, I noticed people had lanterns and were waiting for the priests to unvest. I was made aware that my priest and several other people were going to drive to a neighboring parish. My curiosity became excitement as I was told it was for the Holy Fire. How amazing is this, that my parish would receive the Holy Fire! When asked if I would like to come, I said "YES." It was drizzling a little bit, but seeing how my two priests Fr. Patrick and Fr. Teodor were prepared with their small lanterns, I could only pray that the translation of the flame would be successful.

I was in the car of Monica Raiman, the utmost sweet woman that I would say without hesitation is family and one of my best friends. Together in the car, I couldn't help but be so excited with her, especially since we were still in the season of Pascha. We even sent a picture to my friend to announce the exciting news!

Monica and Simeon on their way to receive the Holy Fire.

We drove to a neighboring ROCOR parish of Holy Epiphany, and the iconography was just breathtaking. There was construction and renovation taking place, but it didn't take away from the grandeur of the iconography. One of the priests of the parish went behind the iconostasis and returned with a small flame lit on a beeswax candle. Can this be the Holy Fire? Fr. Patrick and Fr. Teodor went forward to light their lanterns, and this was enough to tell me it was.

As we said farewell, it was only 30 seconds later as we walked to the cars that one of the lanterns went out! Lord have mercy! One of our priests quickly returned inside and relit it. We drove back and such is the miracle that we received the Holy Fire that day!

Fr. Patrick and Fr. Teodor lighting their lanterns.

85

Icons of the Entrance of the Theotokos into the Temple and the Dormition of the Theotokos.

The iconostasis of Holy Epiphany Orthodox Church.

At this point in time, never would I have imagined I would be driving across America carrying a flame to other churches, let alone nearly 5000 miles. Even before Pascha, my good friend Joseph was going to be driving across America with his car because of his new job in California. It did not take long before we decided that this could be our post-graduation road trip.

Eventually, it was near the end of April that I found the Facebook page for the distribution of the Holy Fire, and then the idea struck me. Immediately I ran to Joseph who lived in the same residence hall as me. I spoke calm and collectedly, just hoping he might say yes. And indeed that was the answer. We were going to bring it across America! At this point I started jumping with joy.

It was agreed that Joseph would plan the route and the locations to visit since it was his road trip after all (the rest of us were just along for the ride). I, on the other hand, was responsible for finding parishes to visit along the route Joseph decided, and to contact the relevant parishes and people who we were to receive the Holy Fire from us. We spent more than several hours deciding which parishes would make the most sense to visit, which was the most practical, and cross referencing this information with parishes on the Holy Fire Map and those that weren't. After thorough planning, I announced the news on the Facebook page. One person responded whether it would be possible for us to drive all the way up to Alaska! They even promised to give us a place to stay when we came! It would have been amazing to have extended the road trip, but I unfortunately had to say no.

I also researched for hours the perfect lanterns we should use. The Facebook group was very helpful in making my decision. Deciding to buy both candle and oil lanterns, with the latter being bought on the first day of our journey at a store, I made the calculations of how many candles we would need. Eventually we made our first order of candle lanterns. In addition, I have to thank the sacristans at my parish, Helen and Diakonissa Mary, for giving me votive candles used at our parish (we keep the flame lit on Pascha throughout the whole year). I didn't have much space in my room, so I left the supplies on my icon corner table, praying that these serve us well on our journey.

Left to right, Raphael, Joseph, Simeon. Photo by Michael Fong.

The trip included Joseph, Raphael and me who are all Orthodox. There was a fourth member as well named Jeffrey, who was not even Christian. He would constantly say that if we got in trouble for carrying a flame, he won't take the blame, and that I better be on top of this whole endeavor. Even though he said this to me before the trip, I give many thanks to him for helping us bring the flame across the country as we shall see later on.

My group would not be driving across the USA until a whole month later, and it was during this time I saw the journey of Dee Kelley unfold on the Facebook group. Seeing that it was very much possible to carry a flame long distance, it gave me further confidence that this was possible. I felt ready to leave that very moment.

Of course, we could not leave until we had graduated! On the morning of my graduation, I had enough time to go to liturgy for St. Nicholas. My Godfather, Deacon Andrey, mentioned that the liturgy would happen, and that it is a great blessing to be able to go to Divine Liturgy (we agreed it's a wonderful way to start any day). Unfortunately, I had extra-curricular work to finish before I left Boston, and I spent the whole night finishing it. By the time I was done, it was only thirty minutes before Liturgy would start. I was very tired, but I had started to read "My

Elder Joseph the Hesychast," which mentioned there is grace given when one prays in the middle of the night, fighting against sleepiness. He described the spiritual life as warfare that requires our 100% devotion and love to our Lord Jesus Christ. I am the farthest thing from a monk, but I thought to myself, perhaps this is an opportunity where I can exert myself a tiny bit to prepare for the trip. Also, it gave me a chance to ask St. Nicholas to aid us in our journey, which we certainly needed!

In addition, this was going to be my last liturgy in Boston before I had to move. Being the parish of my baptism, the community here is very much a part of my real family, so this parish holds near and dear to my heart. How could I possibly miss the chance to go to liturgy before I had to leave!

 Simeon Spencer Kwon
May 23

Christ is Risen!!! The pilgrimage starts. St. Katherina, St. Nicholas, St. John Maximovitch, St. Simeon, St. Joseph, St. Raphael of Brooklyn, and our guardian angels, keep us safe on our journey!

The lit candles from Holy Resurrection and the first Facebook post on our journey!

Our icon corner in Washington DC.

The morning the day after our graduation, my friends and I were all packed and ready to go. Of course, we couldn't possibly leave without the Holy Fire! We agreed to have breakfast a block away from the church while I went to Holy Resurrection to pick up the flame with the lanterns. Considering they run an Orthodox School at Holy Resurrection, all the children said hi to me as I went to light the flame. Once I lit the candles, I was ready to leave.

We were quite squished in a small Honda Fit with four people and their luggage. By the grace of God, we finally arrived at Washington DC on May 23. Immediately I went inside our hotel and set up extra candles just in case, as well as my icons of the Mother of God and St. John Maximovitch. Joseph brought an icon of Christ (and a small one of his patron saint to be kept near his bed).

The next day, we had a bit of time to explore Washington DC. It was quite a wonderful place with monuments and museums. Of course, we soon had to leave for the long ride to Knoxville TN, which would take over seven hours.

The Washington Monument

Jeffrey driving with Raphael in the passenger seat.

As we approached Knoxville, I posted online how we've made it this far. I immediately got a response asking us to come to St. George Greek Orthodox Church. We didn't plan on distributing the fire here because we had activities planned with a friend of ours, Luisa (whose place we were staying at). Raphael mentioned that to be honest, he wished to go to Ascension liturgy if the schedule allowed (as did I). I let my friends know of the invitation, and I stated how unfortunate it is we will have to say no. Joseph's response however was that with the predicted weather, our plans will be cancelled for the next day. Now with the time we had, and by God's grace, Raphael and I had the opportunity to bring the flame to that parish.

After liturgy during a small repast, some asked whether we were financially supported for this trip. I said we were not, as this was a trip we planned anyways even before the Holy Fire arrived. Some insisted that we take a little bit of cash to help us on our journey, especially the elderly. I said we didn't need it, but their insistence could not be overcome, and I thank them that they wanted to help us any way they can. It was so wonderful to go to Ascension liturgy while we shared the flame with them.

The Holy Fire being distributed at St. George Greek Orthodox Church.

The day after Ascension, it was time to move on to our next destination. In Birmingham AL, we checked into the hotel, went out to eat dinner, and returned. I said I would go in first to check the flame. As I walked to the front entrance, a man who was bleeding from the mouth approached me. He said that "I was him" who had punched him in the face. I said that I was not, and that I was just a visitor to Birmingham. He insisted that I was "him" and told me to give him my wallet or else he would beat me up. Knowing that the donation money from the previous church was in my wallet, I kept saying that perhaps we can call the ambulance or police to help him. My friends then came over worried, and the man then asked whether they were with me. They said yes, and he backed off, saying that I wasn't "him." We said we can call the police and he agreed. The police came only thirty seconds later since the man at the front desk of the motel contacted the police much earlier (supposedly the man was harassing someone else). The police arrived in no time and let us go. The man said someone in the hotel punched him in the face, but unfortunately the police said they could not help him unless the man would give him his name for the report. The police realized they couldn't help him unless they had his name, and told him there was nothing they could do then. As the police left, the man continued to stay outside the hotel, saying he "knew you were up there." We agreed to move to a different hotel.

Driving on our way to Mobile AL, and arriving at Annunciation Greek Orthodox Church.

It was quite a scary experience, and I know that surely it was through the intercession of St. Nicholas that I was safe. I just hope the man is okay, and that his injury is taken care of. After all, our Lord commands us to love our enemies.

After spending a day in Birmingham at the Civil Rights Institute, we continued on to Mobile AL. Here we had the pleasure of going to Annunciation Greek Orthodox Church. Although we were thirty minutes late, several people were all patiently waiting for our arrival. Amazingly, they've had their own parish paschal flame running for the last thirty years, which they finally extinguished now that they received the Holy Fire. We were then invited to dinner by Fr. Elias. It was an amazing seafood dinner. When the waitress asked Raphael whether he wanted his shrimp fried or not, Fr. Elias answered on his behalf with a serious "fried."

During dinner, he got a call from the secretary of the church. What happened was she brought the flame home with her husband only for the flame to blow out. With smoke trails coming from the candle, she called to her husband what had happened. As he came into the room, he responded "what are you talking about, it's still lit." She turned around and found the candle still lit, even though seconds ago it was surely extinguished. As per Fr. Elias's words, she was 'hysterical.' Truly it was a miracle of God.

Fr. Elias and the parishioners who were waiting for us.

The beautiful iconography of Annunciation Greek Orthodox Church.

Raphael with his 'fried' shrimp dinner and a group photo with Fr. Elias.

As we said our goodbyes, we returned to our hotel. Because I wanted to have perfectly clean lanterns every day, it was definitely a lot of effort to spend an hour every night cleaning the excess wax off the candle lanterns. Even so, it was enjoyable cleaning such an interesting contraption of a candle lantern.

The next day, we came to New Orleans LA. We were supposed to spend a day in the tourist parts of the city. Just in case, I lit a small votive candle on the floor of the car, praying that the fire is still lit when we return. I also carried the oil lantern with me in the city, but I was very anxious either way since we were tasked to bring the flame all the way to California to Joseph's home parish. We sort of took turns carrying the lantern as we walked around the magnificent tourist city. One time, I was standing by the curb leaning on a rail while my friends were eating (I wasn't hungry). A photographer walked by and stopped to take a picture of me. What will the picture be used for I wonder.

After a long day, we finally decided to go back to the car to check in to our motel. Just ten meters away from the car, the oil lantern went out! I ran to the Honda Civic, praying that the votive candle was still lit. It was, but I was worried about how windy it just became (which is why the lantern went out). The flame of the votive candle was so small, I knew a small draft as we opened the doors could blow it out (especially from some of the stories I read on the Facebook group). I waited for the wind to momentarily subside as I squeezed myself in the car through the slightly open door. I entered the backseat instead of the front where the votive candle was, just to be extra cautious of draft of the car door. It must have been over one hundred degrees in the car, and immediately I started sweating, both from the heat and the immense concentration of meticulously moving the votive candle from the floor of the passenger seat to the back seat. A significant amount of the votive candle was melted, leaving a lot of liquid wax to slosh around and possibly extinguish the fire, and it didn't help either that the flame was very small at this point. Doing all my actions slowly over the course of several minutes, I finally lit the oil lantern with the votive candle. Hallelujah! Giving the thumbs up that we are good, the group entered the car and gently closed the car doors. Immediately the tiniest flame of the votive candle blew out from the draft. This was indeed a close one!

The next day, we arrived at Holy Trinity Greek Orthodox Cathedral in New Orleans for Sunday liturgy. It was such a massive and beautiful church. Fr. George, Presbytera Harriet, their daughter Despina, and Demetrios were all so welcoming. It was also the day of their Greek Festival, so it was such a wonderful break from the last couple stressful days.

Fr. George receiving the Holy Fire from Simeon. Photo by Despina.

We didn't have a church to visit the next few days, and we visited Houston and Dallas TX. It was definitely an eye-opener when we visited the Johnson Space Center with their massive space shuttles. It was also because I knew someone who worked on one of the Apollo missions. We also hiked in Palo Duro Canyon State Park, which was absolutely beautiful to be surrounded by nature for miles.

Group photo of the parish community with Joseph and Raphael in the back.

Later on our journey, we entered New Mexico to meet on May 31st two parties, Elizabeth at the Valley of Fire State Park entrance at 2 PM and a host family in Socorro for All Saints Orthodox Church in Albuquerque. At 1:30, we decided to have lunch only a few minutes from the entrance of the park. As we walked to our car, a huge gust of wind came and extinguished all of our lanterns. At that very moment, I felt as if I couldn't make sense of things. Upset and frantic, I gave a call to Elizabeth a few minutes before 2 PM telling her of the unfortunate news. It broke my heart that she drove hours to get here only to be sent back without the flame.

I then immediately got in the car to find on the Holy Fire map the nearest church with the flame. We found north of us in Los Alamos St. Job of Pochaiv Orthodox Church. I gave them a call with no response. Joseph then put his phone up against the window to show me their service schedule. They had vespers at 5:30 that very day! And this was a Wednesday as well. It was three hours away, and we would arrive perfectly before vespers. We started the car to go to St. Job of Pochaiv Orthodox Church, and Jeffrey knew how much it mattered to me that we relight our lanterns. He said that "even if we had to go back to Texas to get the flame, we should because people are counting on us." Considering he held the lantern for us

Our drive to St. Job of Pochaiv Orthodox Church to relight our candles and lanterns.

on several occasions and helped us carry candles, I cannot be more thankful. He contributed when we needed him, and I definitely owe many thanks to him for all his help.

It didn't take long before I got the call back from the parish inviting us to relight out lanterns. However, it was to my surprise Fr. Theophan Mackey.

Now why was I surprised? Before I left Boston, I planned and contacted the churches and persons in advance. I was initially in touch with Fr. Theophan to share the Holy Fire with his parish along our journey. It was right as we left Boston that he said we did not need to give him the flame because they were going to receive the fire up north in Colorado on their own, presumably spreading from Dee Kelley's journey. When our fire went out, it is amazing that they were the closest parish with the Holy Fire, and also having vespers on Wednesday evening right as we arrived, ensuring they were available at the church to relight our lanterns. They were also kind enough to give us an extra red lantern to aid us on our journey. Instead of them receiving the fire from us, we were the ones receiving the fire from them. Truly this is the work of the providence of God.

Our lantern with the Holy Fire in front of St. Job of Pochaiv Orthodox Church.
Glory to God!

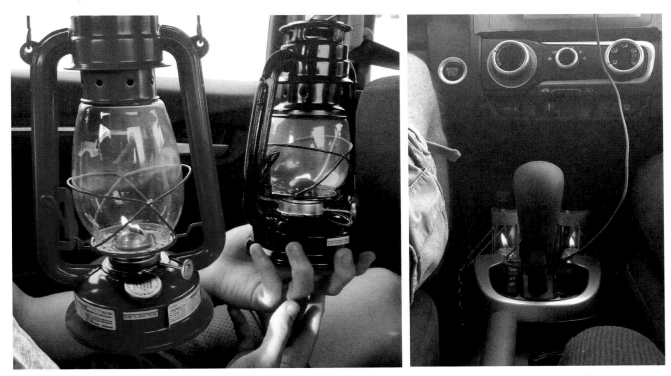

Our lanterns ready to go. The large red lantern courtesy of Fr. Theophan.

One funny story occurred as we arrived. Fr. Theophan was talking to what seemed like inquirers. As we received a blessing from Fr. Theophan by kissing his hand, they asked "why are they kissing your wedding ring?" He responded that he is blessing us, and that it is not his own blessing, but Christ who is doing the blessing through the priest. The woman responded "if so, then can you bless the skin blemish on my neck!" I couldn't help but chuckle at their earnestness, and I wish them the best as they learn about Orthodoxy.

The drive to and from Fr. Theophan's church had a massive elevation change with a beautiful view. We then arrived at the residence of Andrei and Elena Zagrai with their children. They all had their candles and lanterns ready. They prepared such a wonderful dinner for all of us. During dinner, I was able to see from my seat the children in the kitchen looking into the votive candles with curiosity and excitement. Seeing a smoke trail I could tell they blew one out by accident! Luckily they were keeping many candles and lanterns (as were we after the incident), and later I found out they were able to bring it safely to All Saints Orthodox Church in Albuquerque the following Sunday. The children were so excited that they played a mini piano recital for us. They were very sweet and considerate. The family even offered us to stay for the night, but we said we already had a place.

As we were about to leave, the children presented a parting gift for us. Besides homemade nut and granola bars they gave us during dinner, the children presented to us a collection of crayon drawings and a handful of lavender flowers they picked personally from their backyard. Those lavender flowers we then kept on the front dashboard next to our icon for the rest of the trip. Especially from the last few days of close calls and incidents and the immense generosity we received from people we've met along the way, I can't help but think this is a journey beyond just ourselves. This is a journey that is only made possible by all the people who took part in this effort. Most of all, none of our endeavors are possible without Christ. For as the scriptures say, "I am the vine, you are the branches. He who abides in me, and I in him, he it is that bears much fruit, for apart from me you can do nothing" (John 15:5, RSV).

Considering we drove a total of over nine hours that day to relight our candles, we were definitely tired by the time we reached the Zagrai family. The next day, we left Socorro refreshed and full of zeal for what is to come.

The crayon drawings that were given to us as a gift.

The House in Show Low

The next day, we were on our way to St. Anthony's Monastery. For lunch, we stopped at a place called The House in Show Low AZ. I found good reviews online, and we were definitely surprised when we found the menu. There were donut burgers and peanut butter and jelly burgers! We asked the waitress her thoughts, and she mentioned the PB&J burger was her favorite. The donuts are received locally, and sometimes they run out of donuts. I felt very tempted to get the donut burger, but instead opted for the regular burger. I will say that I have never had a better burger than here before. So delicious, that if I was still hungry, I would have tried the donut burger.

The absolutely beautiful weather we had on our way to St. Anthony's Monastery.
The lavender was from the Zagrai children.

We left Show Low AZ, and at this point was only a few hours away from St. Anthony's Monastery. My dear Godmother Margarita always mentions to me to go to Elder Ephraim's Monasteries if I get the chance to. She met Elder Ephraim once, and her description of him as a humble monk is very vivid in my mind. Knowing we would pass through Arizona during our planning stages, I got Joseph to agree it was a great idea to stop by at St. Anthony's Monastery. Also, it just felt appropriate since I was reading "My Elder Joseph the Hesychast" during the trip. I just felt so blessed to finally have arrived at St. Anthony's Monastery, truly an oasis in the desert.

Since Tawfiq Zananiri was very close to the monastery, he let the monastery know on my behalf that we would be bringing the flame. As we passed by the front gate, I could see one of the monks take out a walkie talkie announcing our arrival. We arrived at the front entrance, and the car behind us parked next to us. The woman in the car, seeing our lantern, asked "is that it," and I happily responded saying "yes it is!"

Simeon lighting people's candles.
Photo by Tawfiq.

One of the monks lighting the lampadas.
Photo by Tawfiq.

There were so many people waiting at the front entrance for the Holy Fire. Tawfiq came forward and introduced himself, being so thankful that we brought the flame. As we walked towards the entrance, the people filled with zeal walked towards us to light their candles before I could bring it to the chapel. We were led by one of the monks and Tawfiq to the chapel, and they soon lit all the lampadas of the chapel with the Holy Fire. Right afterwards, there was a service where everyone held candles with the Holy Fire. I just took in the beautiful image of the nave filled with so many candles burning with the Holy Fire.

We were then led to the refectory, where we were to eat our dinner. Another man, Tawfiq's close friend, told me to go to the table in the very front where the Elders sat, and that I should put my candle lantern with the flame on the table. I was so nervous going up, while Tawfiq's close friend told me it was perfectly fine. As I went forward, Elder Paisios just motioned with his hand to put the lantern on the table. After putting down the candle, I returned to my seat, thinking to myself that this was the first time I've ever seen an elder.

Afterwards, I was then led to the nearby home of Tawfiq's friend. They invited me inside with Raphael as they let us bring our lanterns to light their candles. They were all so kind, and Tawfiq's close friend even insisted that I take with me the burning bush from Mount Sinai. I couldn't believe what I was hearing! It turns out Tawfiq's friend went to St. Katherine's Monastery near Mount Sinai and was able to bring a small portion of the burning bush to grow in his garden. It grew to a massive size, more than twice my height and growing over the wall of his garden. They cut off a small portion of the bush with roots, and gave me the burning bush in a pot of soil. I couldn't be more grateful, but they even gave me a small copy of the Hawaii Iveron Icon of the Mother of God with a small vial containing myrrh from the icon itself. To be honest, I have no words to describe their generosity and kindness.

They then drove me back to the monastery, and we were greeted by the monks at the gate. We showed our lantern as he did the sign of the cross. As we continued on, I was told that monk in particular was very excited when it arrived, but had to wait as he was the gatekeeper. As we arrived at the front entrance, a woman asked whether I was Simeon. Turns out it was Laura Ross herself, whom I was in contact

Laura Ross with her lantern and the Holy Fire.

Tawfiq and Simeon, finally meeting each other at St. Anthony's Monastery.

St. Anthony's is truly a desert monastery.

In the evening, it was just so peaceful and quiet.

with on the Facebook group! I helped set up her lanterns and lit her votive candles. As I said goodbye to her, I wished her the best on her own journey of spreading the Holy Fire to nearby parishes.

I will give many thanks to Tawfiq who has done so much preparing our welcome and also delivering the flame to St. Paisius Monastery and other churches in Arizona.

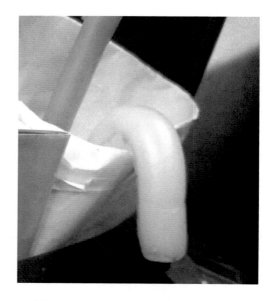

How hot it must have been.

One curious thing I found out was that Jeffrey couldn't fall asleep. He wanted to smoke a cigarette, but he was told he couldn't do so on the monastery grounds. So he walked all the way to the gate of the monastery to light his cigarette. There was a monk at the gate that kept Jeffrey company, and I wonder what conversation they had.

The next day, we prepared to leave with the flame. The inside of our car was so hot, that one of our candles started drooping downwards. We then drove north to the Grand Canyon, and it was definitely a beautiful place to visit.

The Grand Canyon in all its glory.

108

Later that night we arrived in Ash Fork Arizona. During dinner, I had the pleasure of meeting Sherie and Mark who took the flame to St. George's Orthodox Church. Once we got to the motel, I started cleaning the candle lanterns while waiting for Xenia. I got several text messages saying they were having car trouble, and if it was too late. Considering the candle lanterns were filled with so much excess wax that needed to be scraped off, I said I was fine however late it was.

Sometime past midnight, Xenia, Herman and their two sons Mark and John finally arrived. As I got the flame to them, they let me into their RV. They said how they were in Ash Fork buying property when they got a call from a fellow friend that "someone named Simeon is going to Ash Fork to deliver the Holy Fire!" After being convinced perhaps it's a sign that they should buy this property, they afterwards contacted me if I could give them the fire. It just so happened that the day I was supposed to arrive was on their four year wedding anniversary!

I set up their lantern for them, and their baby John kept walking through my legs going back and forth between Herman and Xenia! He was very adorable. As I was about to take a picture of them, their other son Mark suddenly woke up. He looked at us, and Herman mentioned how I had come to share with them the Holy Fire. Mark just stared at us for a few seconds, then immediately dropped his head back into the pillows. Clearly he was tired!

The last group of parishes we were going to was all in California, the first of which was St. Anthony's Parish in San Diego. We arrived on the morning of Pentecost that Sunday, and we could see the church was filled with people, all quiet and trying to get a glimpse of the lanterns as we walked through the narthex. Fr. John came forth with a tiny candle, lighting the votive candles in Christ's tomb. After putting our own lanterns in the tomb and on the altar, a procession was held. How joyous it was, especially because it was the Great Feast of Pentecost! Interestingly, the tiny candle mentioned was a candle Fr. John had for many years even before he was Orthodox. The candle was from the Holy Sepulchre and was originally lit with the Holy Fire. Since then, he kept it and eventually entered the Church to become an Orthodox priest. It was absolutely amazing to have come here for Pentecost, having met Jeanette and Lorinda who contacted me to come here. What I will remember most however is Fr. John's homily, reminding us what

Sherie and Mark Mercier with their lantern, with several more in the car as well.

Xenia and Herman with their son John. Mark is asleep in the back.

Fr. John and his homily, teaching the children how to keep alive the Holy Fire and the fire in our hearts.

is truly important, even more than the Holy Fire itself. Fr. John said just as we must protect the flame of the Holy Fire, we must also keep alive the fire in our hearts. There are three things we must do to keep both fires alive he said. We must protect it, feed it, and trim it.

When he asked the children how we can protect the Holy Fire, the children answered we have to protect the flame from wind, knocking the candle over, and according to one child, from little sisters! Fr. John said the fire within us must be protected similarly, but from dark things of the world that may try to extinguish the flame. We have to feed the flame or else it will run out of fuel. We refill the oil lamps and add more candles. So too do we feed our flame with Holy Communion, praying, reading scripture, going to church, and almsgiving. And lastly, we must trim the wick. We must take care of the wick of an oil lamp for example, or else soot builds up that may hinder the flame. Likewise we trim the wick of our flame time to time, offering up to God our sins in confession to maintain that burning fire in us. We then said our goodbyes, feeling ever so blessed to have come here for Sunday liturgy.

The wonderful parish community of St. Barnabas Orthodox Church.

That same day, we then stopped at St. Barnabas Orthodox Church to light their candles. We planned to meet another parish at 4 PM, so we weren't able to stay too long.

The third parish we were to meet on Pentecost was Joy of All Who Sorrow in Culver City. Upon entering, I realized how many people were waiting for us inside. Candles were lit, and one woman, truly touched that the Holy Fire was brought there, asked me many times to pray for her family. Even early on in the trip, I received a video announcing the arrival of the Holy Fire in Culver City. They were all so excited!

I really felt all the love and anticipation these people had for us as we brought the flame. There was one girl who came up to me several times because she kept blowing out her candle by accident!

The Holy Fire arrives in Culver City! Photo by Matushka Deborah Tomasi.

They had a small service led by Fr. John Tomasi, and my goodness it was amazing to be in a room filled to the brim with everyone holding a candle. At the end, Fr. John yelled as loud as he could "The Holy Spirit has descended" with just as loud of a response "from Heaven to Earth!"

I had such a wonderful time speaking with Matushka Deborah Tomasi and to finally meet Theophan Lujan and Angelica Sotiriou, whom I was in contact with during the journey. Angelica had to leave quite early to bring the flame to her parish, but she gave me a wonderful gift before leaving. She gave me a prayer book and a cross, which I wear every day.

Simeon relighting a girl's candle. Photo by Theophan Lujan.

113

Fr. John as he starts the service. Photo by Theophan Lujan.

A beautiful picture of the Holy Fire. Photo by Theophan Lujan.

Fr. John as he yells "The Holy Spirit has Descended!" Photo by Theophan Lujan.

Angelica Sotiriou lighting her lanterns before she had to leave. Photo by Theophan Lujan.

Group photo before we had to leave.

On our way to Mountain View CA, we had a chance to visit Joseph's brother's Godparents, Mr. and Mrs. Fetzko. We didn't think of it until that day, but we asked whether they would want to receive the Holy Fire for their parish, Orthodox Church of the Annunciation. They said yes!

Mr. and Mrs. Fetzko with the Holy Fire.

We finally arrived on June 6th to Joseph's house in Mountain View CA. It was a long journey, but by the prayers of the saints and God's grace, we finally reached our final destination. There was however one more parish to visit, which is none other than Church of the Redeemer in Los Altos CA, the home parish of my good friend Joseph. Mr. and Mrs. Stroud, Joseph's parents were wonderful hosts to Raphael, Jeffrey and me. We had time to rest after this pilgrimage of sorts, which we definitely appreciated.

Orthodox Church of the Annunciation receives the Holy Fire!

Church of the Redeemer! Our final destination.

During this time, we were able to visit both the old and new Russian cathedrals in San Francisco, both which are connected to St. John Maximovitch. The icon of St. John I had during the journey was from the newer cathedral and supposedly touched his relics. Knowing St. John was helping us on our journey, I just had to collect myself once I was in front of his relics. I venerated his relics, thinking to myself that in front of me are the relics of a real saint. There is not much to say on this, except that the saints are truly our magnificent friends in heaven, persons who we can cherish as our intercessors before God.

On June 11th, we took the lanterns to the final destination, Church of the Redeemer. It was Sunday liturgy, and Fr. Samer told us to come exactly at a specified time during matins, which was when they would chant "Having beheld the Resurrection of Christ." He took the lanterns into the altar area and came forward with a lit candle. One man then came forth with a torch of smaller candles and had them all lit, candles which were also lit with the Holy Fire at the Holy Sepulchre many years ago. In the narthex, everyone began to light their own candles with the Holy Fire.

Everyone lights their candles in the narthex.

Fr. Samer lighting more candles at the end of Divine Liturgy.

The absolutely incredible iconography.

As my host family told me, many of the parishioners here used to live near or in the Holy Land. Many were able to personally visit the Lord's tomb and witness the Holy Fire personally when they were growing up, and they were just so thankful we were bringing back to them memories of their homeland.

This church has an amazing story attached behind it as well. The church with the beautiful iconography was actually built after the church burned down from arson in 2002. No one knew who committed such an act, but what remained in the ashes was a reminder from God in this tumultuous time. What remained from the altar was the Gospel book with one unburnt page reading: "You have heard that it was said, 'An eye for an eye and a tooth for a tooth.' But I say to you, Do not resist one who is evil. But if anyone strikes you on the right cheek, turn to him the other also; and if anyone would sue you and take your coat, let him have your cloak as well; and if anyone forces you to go one mile, go with him two miles" (Matthew 5:38-41). Truly a message from God, it reminds us that when we face opposition, persecution, and evil, we do not return the same but instead the love of Christ.

The remains of the fire were left in a glass display case. As you can see, God had a message for these people.

The burning bush growing in my backyard.

A couple days later, it was then my turn to leave. Packing with me the burning bush and my icons, I went home. I planted the burning bush in my backyard, which at this point is growing very well.

The entire experience, going from church to church, travelling and meeting new people, reminds me of "The Way of the Pilgrim." By no means am I the same pilgrim in the book. I had a car, air conditioning, assurance of food and water, a place to sleep every night, and everything opposite of the ascetical journey of the pilgrim. Even so, I remember my bishop speaking to me about the lives of ascetics who lived the angelic life. Not everyone can do the things they do, but that doesn't mean we can't live the angelic life in our own small way. Doing a small good deed, fasting on Wednesdays and Fridays, doing prayers for just a few minutes every night, my bishop says is still very valuable. And so in a way, perhaps we and everyone else in America who took the responsibility of spreading the Holy Fire are pilgrims as well.

But pilgrims in a sense are never alone. Just as the pilgrim met many people on his journey, so do we. We are more than just individuals. During the journey, I witnessed our Orthodox brothers and sisters from many different places, of all walks of life, coming together in Christ. As much as they are thankful to my group and me, I cannot help but also express the same gratitude and thanks to everyone I've met on this trip. It was humbling, and surely an experience that strengthens my faith for the future to come. The Holy Fire is truly a miracle of God, but equally so are all the fellow Orthodox brothers and sisters, for together we make up the Body of Christ.

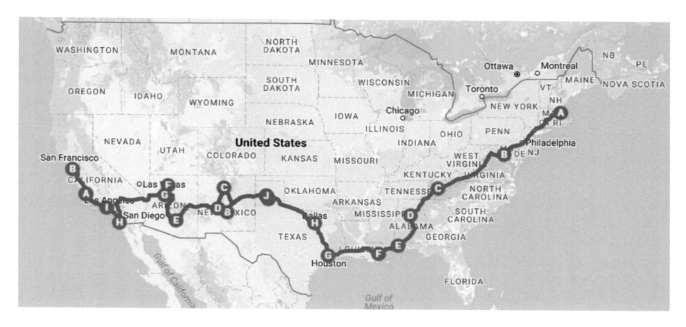

The route from start to finish.

1. Allston, MA – Holy Resurrection Orthodox Church

2. Washington DC

3. Knoxville, TN – St. George Orthodox Church

4. Birmingham, AL

5. Mobile, AL – Annunciation Greek Orthodox Church

6. New Orleans, LA – Holy Trinity Greek Orthodox Cathedral

7. Houston, TX

8. Dallas, TX

9. Palo Duro Canyon State Park

10. Amarillo, TX

11. Valley of Fires

12. Los Alamos, NM – relight at St. Job of Pochaiv Orthodox Christian Church

13. Socorro, NM – host family for All Saints Orthodox Church

14. Florence, AZ – St. Anthony's Monastery

15. Grand Canyon

16. Ash Fork, AZ – Sherie Mercier and Xenia Danielle

17. San Diego, CA – St. Anthony the Great Orthodox Church

18. Costa Mesa, CA – St. Barnabas Orthodox Church

19. Culver City, CA – Joy of All Who Sorrow Orthodox Church

20. Santa Monica, CA

21. Santa Maria, CA – family for Orthodox Church of the Annunciation

22. San Luis Obispo, CA

23. Mountain View, CA

24. Los Altos, CA – Church of the Redeemer

IV

Other Stories

Sasha Gajewski

On April 23, 2017, I was on Facebook, and saw a picture in my newsfeed of a family friend who was travelling home with the Holy Fire. I was in awe and curious how and where she got it. The very next day, while browsing my newsfeed, a parish nearby, All Saints Greek Orthodox Church in Canonsburg, PA, received the Holy Fire! Again, I was in awe, and completely amazed that this church received the Holy Fire, but this time it was nearby! My immediate thought was to call Fr. George Livanos, and ask if I could receive the Holy Fire to bring to my parish and home.

Soon after I saw his post on Facebook, I came across the Facebook group - Come Receive the Holy Fire! and joined. I was immediately given the name of someone nearby, who had the Holy Fire, and could possibly meet. Lisa Ryan from St. Peter and St. Paul Ukrainian Orthodox Church in Carnegie, PA offered to meet me, and she also gave me advice on how to transport the Holy Fire to my home. She suggested that I take 2 candles (a 6 or 7 day candle or lantern), and a taper in case I needed to re- light one if the flame blew out. I was a bit ambitious, and did all of this rather quickly, but finally contacted my parish priest Fr. Thomas Soroka. He was thrilled, and so kind to allow me to be the one to bring the Holy Fire to my parish to distribute at Great Vespers. He quickly sent an email out to our parish explaining the wonderful news! "Saturday at 5:00pm, we will receive the Holy Fire which descends in a miraculous way yearly at the Lord's Sepulcher in Jerusalem on Holy Saturday."

This year is the first year that the Holy Fire has been brought overseas to our shores. Thanks to the kindness of Alexandra Gajewski, she will bring the Holy Fire to Vespers to share with all of us which she will receive through the grassroots network of pious Orthodox believers. We will all share in this blessing during the service as we hold lit candles which will take their flame directly from the Holy Fire."

On April 28th, my husband and daughter were able to come with me to receive the Holy Fire. I was delighted that we would be able to share this once in a lifetime experience together as a family. It seemed so quick and easy. We met Lisa, exchanged Paschal greetings, she lit my lantern, and off we went. I couldn't quite comprehend the significance of what just happened. I was holding the Holy Fire! I was smiling from ear to ear, too nervous about safely bringing the Holy Fire to our home 15 minutes away. When we got home, we had several lampadas ready, and placed the Holy Fire by our icon corner. The flame of the beautiful oil lamp was so pure and white, and still. We needed to keep the Holy Fire going for at least a day, until we had to bring the Holy Fire to Great Vespers at my parish, Saint Nicholas Orthodox Church in McKees Rocks, PA.

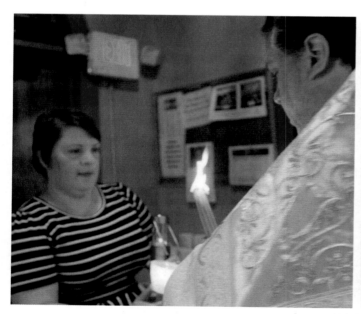

Fr. Thomas receiving the fire and lighting a woman's candles.

Fr. Thomas distributing the Holy Fire to the altar boys.

It was time for us to get ready and leave for Great Vespers. I didn't think about what a challenge it would be to travel with the Holy Fire. Even though we had planned to leave early, we were still rushed, and managed to forget our taper candle. All we had was a small lantern, and a 6 day candle. We live in Pittsburgh, so we had to drive down steep hills, potholes, and brick roads at times. The drive was only 15 minutes, but it seemed like hours. Within 5 minutes of leaving our house, we hit a small bump on the road, and the flame in the lantern blew out. I was worried about disappointing my parish if I was not able to get the Holy Fire there, but I was determined, and we made it after quite a bumpy ride. We sat in the car for a few minutes talking about how we wanted to handle bringing in the flame, since we only had one lit candle. We were afraid that if we opened the door, the flame would blow out. We decided to have my husband go into the church and get a taper, so that we could re-light the lantern. It worked, and I slowly walked into church with the 6 day candle and lantern.

Father Thomas with the Holy Fire.

Father Thomas was ready for me, and when I opened the church door, he immediately came over to me in the Narthex with a bundle of candles, lit them and distributed them to our congregation. 50 people attended Great Vespers that evening. I felt so relieved that I was able to get the Holy Fire to them. So many people thanked me for bringing it to our parish, and some had tears in their eyes. Many people tried to bring the Holy Fire home, some made it, and some didn't. I couldn't have done it without the help of my family, and I am deeply blessed to have been able to share the Holy Fire with others, and to have it in my own home.

Angelica Sotiriou-Rausch

Simeon Kwon was the wonderful young man that took the trek and brought us the Holy Fire. It was truly a miracle that it made it to our parishes. I was one of the three emissaries that picked up the Holy Fire from Joy of All Who Sorrow in Culver City to bring the Holy Fire to my parish, Saint Katherine Greek Orthodox Church in Redondo Beach California. We made it just in time and brought the Holy Fire to our Pentecost Kneeling Service at 6pm on June 4, 2017. It was miraculous. We are indebted to Simeon Kwon for his tenacity in protecting and delivering the Holy Fire to both communities.

Robert Gibson

It was a Wednesday evening, we approached the Church in anticipation, not too many people were there yet. The nave was empty, perhaps if we tried the social hall. As we descended the stairs, voices rose to meet us. We rounded the corner and there was Father Jonathan with several members of his congregation. I approached, "Father Bless" I said with cupped hands. Having received his blessing I continued, "we've met before and you know of my uncle, Father Luke." "Of course," he replied with a warm smile, and then spying the lamps my girls were holding, he added "You're here for the fire? Right this way." We followed him back up the stairs into the nave.

Christ the Redeemer Carpatho-Russian Orthodox Church in Rockford, Illinois is small, but beautifully appointed. The fire was at the front just off the ambon and to the right. Father Jonathan Bannon took a long match, lit it from the candle with the Holy Fire, and while I held my lamps open he lit them.

Robert Gibson and Fr. Jonathan Bannon.

During this time the nave began to fill, he invited us to stay for the service and the refreshments after. As we sang prayers and songs of worship to our God I was filled with wonder at the flame in the lanterns by our legs. I felt lifted up by the flame which had come all the way from Jerusalem, from the very tomb of our Lord. Yet the weight of the responsibility now on my shoulders was present too. We had volunteered to bring this precious flame back to our own Church. Do we have enough oil, will the lamps stay lit? Will the lamps get too hot? Will the fumes be too much? All these questions danced before me. After the service and some food we thanked Father Jonathon and took our leave. It was then the first question came into prominence. Do we have enough oil? We had not done much, if anything, with oil lamps before this. We had anticipated lighting the lamps at the end of the service, not the beginning. So, we didn't know how long it would yet last. The decision was made to stop at my uncle's home to refill the lamps. Father Luke greeted us at the door, welcomed us in, and allowed us to use his sink to hold the lamps while we refilled them.

Reassured, we visited for a while with Father Luke and Matushka Miriam and continued on our way. As we traveled through the dark, my wife took a picture of our daughters' faces glowing in the light of the Holy Fire and I found myself

Arabel and Jadyn Gibson in the car, and the lanterns after we arrived home.

Our icon corner with the Holy Fire.

wondering what other drivers might think of this vehicle going down the road lit on the inside with fire. That was the first time, but not the last, when it occurred to me how separate we are, "in the world, but not of it" as it is written. We knew the significance of our errand, but how many around us did not.

We arrived home safely with the flame and lit our larger oil lamp. Again we were faced with the prospect of what we didn't know, would the flame last the night, would an unattended flame be safe. What about the fumes? I wish I could say we faced all the questions with faith. Instead, we slept with the windows open and arose in the night to check the flame several times. But first, and despite our doubts, we lit the candles in our icon corner that night with the Holy Flame and our prayers basked in its radiance.

The next morning gave us two tasks, one to prepare to keep the flame ourselves and the other to take the flame to our church, St. Ignatius Antiochian Orthodox Church in Fitchburg, Wisconsin. We had determined by the fumes from the lamp the night before that we wanted to switch to candles. This led to other questions, could the glass become too hot and damage a surface on which it sat? Could the glass itself break towards the end and again could we trust the candle at home unattended or overnight? With the help of our fellow Orthodox on the "Come Receive the Holy Fire!" Facebook page we decided to move ahead and purchased several multi-day candles from nearby store. Of course as any of you who have used multiday devotional candles will know, none of our fears materialized, though it took us a few days to figure that out.

Having committed ourselves to that course at home, we undertook our second challenge, and I again loaded our oil lamps into cans, this time in my car for the journey north to Church. As I traveled, the uneventful trip gave me time to reflect again. It was a work day, but I was not at work having taken the day off; I was part of something more. While people rushed on around me wrapped up in their day to day lives I was participating in a miracle that swept aside time and space. I was transporting flame that crossed oceans and continents, and not only me; I was one of a community of others doing the same thing. I was participating in a miracle, in a line of miracles going back at least 16 centuries that had now found its way here. I pulled up to our church and paused to take a picture of the flame against the back drop of the church and then proceeded inside. There, I delivered the flame to our priest Father Basil Koory, who took it from the lamp and lit a candle which he placed among the relics, a fitting place for it to be. From that flame, now many others have been lit and so the story continues, and so are we all joined in one experience, in one community, in one faith, just as Orthodoxy is meant to be.

The Holy Fire arriving at our parish with Fr. Basil Koory.

Brandi Fraysur

I am so humbled, astounded and amazed that the Holy Fire has come, not only to my country and state, but to my own parish as well. I will never be able to express how much this means to me. What makes it so significant to me is that it was only a few months ago in October of 2016 that my son and I almost died during his premature labor. It was only by God's grace, prayers, and the teachings of the Orthodox Church that saved us. I literally felt my spirit leave my body and, when I couldn't call out with my voice, the Icon of Christ helped me

I receive the Holy Fire.

focus and cry out to God with my whole heart. Our prayers were heard and our lives were saved that day. Then the Holy Fire was received at our church on Mother's Day! It could not have been a more meaningful day for me and it will always be etched on my heart. God's love and power is astounding. May the Holy Fire of Orthodoxy continue to spread across this country, the eternal flame that can never be extinguished.

Ready to bring the Holy Fire home.

The Holy Fire in the car, and eventually at home.

Oklahoma's Orthodox faithful help keep 'holy fire' alive

The spreading of the Holy Fire appears in the newspaper, as "Oklahoma's Orthodox faithful help keep 'holy fire' alive."

Fr. Phillip

We received the Holy Fire around 11:00 PM on Sunday night May 7, 2017 in a parking lot in northeast Calgary from John Petkau (long white moustache and beard) and Jack Hill who are both from Edmonton and had been down to Missoula to pick it up. The photographs show us meeting and receiving the Holy Fire. Regrettably, my wife, Matushka Barbara Eriksson was not in any of the pictures because she was taking them all.

Matushka Barbara and I drove the Holy Fire to our church, Holy Martyr Peter the Aleut Orthodox Church and lit a seven day candle which is sitting on the Epitaphios in our building. There are pictures of the receiving, transportation and arrival at our church as well as pictures of the transfer of the fire to the lantern in which it burns. We have the fire burning in multiple locations, in case one of them goes out, we are able to restore the flame from the other candle.

It has been a joy to us to have received this blessed touch of God's grace here in Calgary.

Fr. Phillip meeting Jack Hill.

Fr. Phillip lighting his green lantern from Jack and John's lantern.

Fr. Phillip and John Petkau.

Fr. Phillip, John and Jack.

Arrived at Holy Martyr Peter the Aleut Orthodox Church.

Finally arrived inside.

Setting down the lantern.

All set up.

More candles.

An icon of Christ's Resurrection

Presvytera Carolyn and Susan Kourpouanides

Susan and Presvytera Carolyn of Ft Myers, Florida start their Journey to receive the Holy Fire.

During the first week of May, the wheels were turning as the Joy of Pascha was continuing. After making connections with Patty Martinovich of Venice, Florida, Presvytera Carolyn Nastos and Susan Kourpouanides of Annunciation Greek Orthodox Church knew they had to obtain the Holy Fire and bring it back to the Faithful of Fort Myers and Southwest Florida. It didn't seem like anyone was starting a path down to Florida. They made the schedule to drive up Highway 75 about an hour to meet Patty and receive the Holy Fire. They also invited the Faithful of Holy Trinity, Port Charlotte, Florida to receive the Fire. They figured how to keep the Fire burning with a 7-day candle in the drink holder and Susan keeping eye over the oil lamp in a bucket in the back seat. They drove cautiously back to Fort Myers Parish and passed the Holy Fire onto Rev. Fr. Dean Nastos and everyone who was waiting for us upon our return. It was spine tingling to see everyone waiting. Monday, May 8th another Service was held at night and even more faithful kept coming to receive the Light - taking them home in whatever candle or oil lamp they could. The Holy Fire remains eternal on the Altar at Annunciation Greek Orthodox Church to this day.

Rev. Fr. Dean Nastos received the Holy Fire from Susan Kourpouanides and Presvytera Carolyn on May 7, 2017.

Nikki Johnson

How did the Holy Fire group and collaborative effort begin?

There was no master plan or great vision or organizational chart or concrete timeline when it started – far from it. It all started with a sincerely asked "what if…?" in an informal online discussion of the news story about the fire's expected sojourn to the North American continent. Ask an Orthodox Hipster, one of the less, shall we say, "serious" Orthodox groups on Facebook, provided the forum, on April 21, 2017, in which the seed of an idea could take root in hearts. Reverend

Father Patrick O'Rourke, Assistant Priest at Holy Trinity Greek Orthodox Church in New Rochelle, NY, was essential to the earliest efforts, because his infectious enthusiasm for the idea and can-do approach made this improbable concept seem possible. Ideas were tossed back and forth in comment form in what grew into a lengthy thread. Someone asked if we could make a map, and fellow group member Nicole Johnson responded by creating what would become the Holy Fire volunteer map on Google maps.

Before too long, Fr. Patrick realized that the project, which now had only a map to help with visualization and a nascent concept of how the effort might work in rough form, needed to break out of the confines of the group where it started. He started the Come Receive the Holy Fire! group, and added Caleb Shoemaker, Alexandra Lukas, Rachael Chaney, and Nicole Johnson to the newly-minted group as administrators. Presvytera Magda Andronache joined as administrator the next day, as the initial logistics were being worked out and the first several members were being added. Once the group was opened to the public, some initial instructions for using the map were posted, and the group began to be shared widely. Within a few days, dozens of members were added to the group and an almost equal number of pins had been posted on the map.

There were a few growing pains in those first busy days. None of the original administrators had any idea of how quickly or widely the idea would spread, or whether the volunteers would actually cooperate to get the fire to each other when it arrived. We didn't know how to do this. Not really. It became clear early on, however, that there was incredible interest in the idea, and that if it were to succeed, this would be an unprecedented event in more ways than one. Not only was the Holy Fire coming to the U.S. for the first time in decades, but it was to be carried effortlessly across jurisdictional lines. Ethnicity and even canonicity were secondary to the joy of spreading of the beautiful miracle of the fire.

Early on, the group faced a bit of a setback. The map was originally open for anyone to edit, and all new members were encouraged to add their own information in order to keep the administrators' workload manageable. That seemed fine, until a map user accidentally, we presume, deleted everybody's names and map pins. Faced with an empty map which previously had about 100

Fr. Christopher Foley of Holy Cross Orthodox Church (OCA) in High Point, NC, leads the faithful in a service upon the arrival of the Holy Fire. Holy Cross is the home parish of the Facebook group administrators Caleb Shoemaker and Nicole Johnson.

annotations of name and place, the administrators started to scramble to recover what had been lost, while reassuring the worried group members who watched our earliest shared efforts disappear. By the grace of God, one administrator had an unrefreshed screen in her computer browser and could still see the lost data, even if it could not be restored to the map automatically. So she began the task of copying the data from every pin into a text document that could be used for reconstruction.

That lesson learned the hard way, the map was then locked down so that only a select group of people who knew how the map functioned could add anything to it, and, perhaps more importantly, delete anything from it! Between the rapid group growth of the group, excited and inquisitive conversation threads to manage, and a map to reconstruct and update continuously, there was simply too much for a few part-time administrators to do. A request was made to group members for tech-savvy volunteers who were passionate about the fire's journey to help with the mounting work. Anna Holdren, Reader Michael Smith, Melissa Kay, Luke Childs, and Presvytera Victoria Moody answered the call. Energized by the presence of these new volunteers, the group administrators finished replacing each lost pin, developed a spreadsheet for back-up, and began adding information for all of the new people who poured in.

From those who faithfully added new members to the group and new data to the map, often at all hours of the day and night, and those who prayed faithfully, to those who excitedly drove with flickering lamps across state and jurisdictional lines, and those who provided encouragement or helped with communication, this was a group effort born of love and faith. All of it was done by rather ordinary laypeople, clergy, and monastics who believed that God could do something extraordinary with the Holy Fire on this continent. After all, the fire itself had come to humanity by miraculous means, before being spread by decidedly ordinary ones. We had this gift given on Pascha at the place of Christ's entombment and glorious third-day resurrection, and it only seemed right to share it. "Christ is Risen!" we proclaimed together, and took into our hearts, hands, cars, homes, and churches the radiant fire of His love and his victory over death itself.

So, how did this effort come together? Some might say "Miraculously!"

Servant of God

I live out of my car, lost everything due to the financial crash years ago, but that is not the story I want to talk about. The story is better than that; it is about being part of something huge, something that has never happened in the US. I was chosen because a church member's flame went out and I had the time to get it from another place. It was nerve-racking, I didn't want to mess up. I made sure I had back up: three candles (one from the dollar store), a seven day candle from church and two lanterns. I almost took the flame across state. It was hilly. I was not sure what I was more worried about, the flame going out or my car not getting up the gorge. The flame went out a few times, except the dollar tree candle, burning my hands and hot wax dripping everywhere, getting lost trying to find the churches, having no other person to help except my Guardian Angel, that never went out. With God's help I was able to deliver the flame to a few churches, as a homeless person. I chose to stay anonymous, even in my own church, because as an Orthodox Christian, I don't want the focus to be on me or my situation, but wanted it to be focused on the greater cause, that is the Holy Flame in the US. It is good to know that our flame is still burning.

The Holy Fire at Holy Cross in High Point, NC.

Epilogue:
Mystery and the Holy Fire

By Fr. Haralambos Spaliatsos
Annunciation Greek Orthodox Church
Missoula, Montana

Is receiving the Holy Fire a miracle?
Is it a blessing?
What are we supposed to do with it?
How do we receive it?
What do we do with it once we have it?

These were just some of the questions people began to ask, and which I myself began to ponder, as news spread that the Holy Fire was making its way to our Orthodox Church in Missoula, Montana. The journey of two members of our community, carrying the Holy Fire 2500 miles from Maryland to Montana, and making over 15 stops along the way, would give us time to prepare to receive this gift and prayerfully contemplate what we were about to receive.

At the end of an evening Paraklesis service nearly two weeks before the Holy Fire arrived, I announced to those in attendance that our sweet David and Dee Kelley were going to be driving the Holy Fire to Missoula, and immediately there was an excitement that began to build. One parishioner, who having grown up in Greece and received the Holy Fire many times, began to cry as I shared the news; with tears pooling in her eyes as she came forward for a blessing, she said, "I had been praying that one day the Holy Fire would come to the United States!" Other parishioners began to ask the questions I mentioned above; all pointing to the reality that this was a first for American Orthodoxy, and that as exciting as it was to know that the continuity of Light was making its way to churches across our country, there was a bit of uncertainty about what it all meant.

The question that I received most was, "What does it mean to receive the Holy Fire?" This first question inevitably led to follow up questions, like, "Is it still a miracle? Is it a blessing? Is it sacramental? Can non-Orthodox take the Holy Fire too? How long do we keep it burning?" All of the questioning made sense as this was a new experience for us all.

The answer I chose, perhaps as Orthodox priests often do with questions that are difficult to answer, was to connect the Holy Fire to the idea of mysteria, or mystery. Remembering that the mysteries of a life in Christ cannot be limited to a mere seven, everything in God's creation has the ability to connect us to our Living God; and every encounter with God is beyond our ability to completely understand, describe, or explain – thus, it is mystery. What we do know is the fire we received was first miraculously received through the loving humility of a bishop who placed his faith in the mystery of God's desire to continually be known by His creation. The Holy Fire, in being received, creates excitement from the moment the Patriarch of Jerusalem makes his way out of the tomb of our Lord, because it is a visible reminder of God's ceaseless desire to be connected with us. Perhaps we, like Thomas, sometimes need to see these miracles, so that our faith may be continually strengthened. The excitement doesn't end as the fire leaves the Church of the Holy Sepulcher, but rather people around the Middle East and Eastern Europe are awaiting and anticipating its spread. To see the light of the flame, to remember from where it came, and to experience both the joy and the peace that comes with the visual confirmation that the Light can never be overtaken by darkness, truly the only words that seem sufficient are the words of proclamation of our Lord's victory: "Christ is Risen!"

It is a miracle! How the Holy Fire appears is miraculous; beyond our ability to understand, describe, or explain. But as the Holy Fire made its way across the United States for the first time, perhaps the greater miracle was in how it touched the lives of so many as it spread. The spread of the Holy Fire reminded us that while oceans may divide us, and while languages and cultural traditions may express our divine work in different ways, in the Holy Spirit, given, seen, and spread through a visible Light of fire, we have the ability to overcome separation and to become one; the one Body of our Lord, God, and Savior, Jesus Christ. This tangible foretaste of our universal unity in Christ is indeed beyond our ability to understand, describe, or explain – it is miraculous…it is mystery.

In Missoula, Montana, we have one Orthodox Church. Americans, Greeks, Antiochians, Romanians, Russians, Serbians, Eritreans, Ethiopians, Moldovans, Italians, Norwegians, Assyrians, Ukrainians, Georgians, and many others, all come together each Sunday to become the Body of Christ, and in becoming, we taste the Kingdom as we receive His Body and Blood. As the Holy Fire made its way into our Church on that Sunday morning in May, as we lifted up the flame for all to see and to receive, as we proclaimed "Christ is risen!" in over 12 languages, and as the joy and peace of the Holy Spirit through this Holy Light filled our hearts, the icon of the kingdom was made more perfectly manifest in the reflection of unity in our diversity. The Holy Light of Christ, made visible through the All-Holy Spirit, uniting, recreating, and transforming us in His divine image. What a miracle! What a mystery!

Fr. Haralambos shares the Holy Fire.

Made in the USA
Middletown, DE
16 February 2023

25025806R00091